Crisis in Eden

• • • • • • • • • • • •

Crisis in Eden

· · · · · · · · · · · ·

a religious study of man and
environment

Frederick Elder

A B I N G D O N   P R E S S
NASHVILLE   NEW YORK

CRISIS IN EDEN

Copyright © 1970 by Abingdon Press

All rights reserved.

ISBN 0-687-09907-2

Library of Congress Catalog Card Number: 75-98896

SET UP, PRINTED, AND BOUND BY THE
PARTHENON PRESS, AT NASHVILLE,
TENNESSEE, UNITED STATES OF AMERICA

to my family
whose support in various ways
helped to make this book possible

Preface

The writer of Psalm 8, gazing in wonder and awe at a Near Eastern night, whispered and later wrote, "O Lord . . . what is man, that thou art mindful of him?" Later, probably no longer under the influence of the star-spangled canopy of the night sky, he would add to this first reverent response with words of a different spirit, saying, "Thou madest him to have dominion over the works of thy hands; thou hast put all things under his feet." (KJV)

In this book I deal with the two contrasting views of nature that are inherent in the respective statements of the psalmist, and the implications of the choice between the two. In my treatment I move

7

into both biblical-theological and scientific areas of investigation, and attempt to show that on the basis of such investigations the first thought of wonder by the psalmist is a better guide for our day than the afterthought of human domination.

Subjugation of nature has been the prevailing view of Western man during the entire Christian era, with roots, as the reference to the psalm indicates, that go back even further. This view has been challenged occasionally, but never effectively counteracted. Now, however, in a day of spiraling population, mounting pollution, and the fear that man is becoming more the object than the subject of control in the world he has built, the need for an effective alternative to the old man-nature alienation and combat is apparent. Through the process of opting for the view of those whom I call the inclusionists—especially as such a view is expressed in the work of Loren Eiseley—and then giving particular Christian expression to such a view, I present at least the outline of such an alternative.

We are on the threshold of a critical period. The overriding question of that period is whether man is going to choose a new path of harmony with nature or will continue down the old road of domination which inevitably leads to some form of his own subjugation. This book is an attempt to influence the choice toward the former and away from the nightmare that lies in the opposite direction.

Acknowledgments

In regard to the formation of this book, I am indebted, first of all, to Daniel Luten of the University of California, Berkeley, whose humble and yet powerful presentation of the ecological point of view first focused the emphasis that is found in my writing.

I am deeply grateful to Loren Eiseley, who was kind enough to inform me that my analysis of his work was essentially correct, and who lent support to my attempt to interpret theologically certain interacting social and biological trends. My thanks also go to Ian McHarg, a fellow faculty member of Eiseley's at the University of Pennsylvania, under whose auspices I received much valuable material. In connection with that material I also want to thank those of the Fine Arts Library and the Department of Landscape Architecture of the University of Pennsylvania for their assistance.

Certainly I extend the deepest gratitude to my faculty leader at Harvard, Arthur Dyck, who patiently advised me in the formation of the thesis on which this book is based. As one very much in tune with a gestalt or comprehensive viewpoint, and as one of the foremost leaders in the Christian examination of population problems, he proved indispensable both in his criticism and his guidance.

Finally, my thanks to my wife, Barbara, who has shared much of the burden and some of the satisfaction connected with the fashioning of this work.

An extract from the thesis on which this book is built has appeared as an essay in the hard-bound volume, *The Religious Situation: 1969,* and the paperback volume, *Updating Life and Death: Essays in Ethics and Medicine,* both published by Beacon Press. The essay is entitled "Two Modern Doctrines of Nature."

Contents

I Introduction

Nature can be understood in at least two contrasting ways. The more common definition of nature is: the physical systems apart from man and his civilization which form man's basic, given environment. It refers to what would be present if man were to somehow disappear from the earth. From this view there arises the general tendency to think in terms of man *and* environment, that is, man standing over against nature. However, there is another definition of nature which is more comprehensive, for it includes man and his works within its compass. From this view there arises the tendency to think in terms of man *in* environment, that is, man as an inextricable part of nature.

These two definitions outline the contrast between the two groups that form the "dialogue" of this study and that present the alternatives open to modern man so far as his relation with the natural order is concerned. The first of these groups we may call the "inclusionists." It is they who are informed by the more comprehensive definition of nature, the ones who include man in the overall consideration and calculus.

This group is largely composed of life scientists —biologists, botanists, anthropologists, ecologists. It also includes certain urban planners and landscape architects. This group is not formally organized, but it is intellectually distinguishable by its holistic approach, that is, by its awareness and elucidation of the interrelated web of all life. It is this approach that binds together a naturalist such as Rachel Carson with a botanist such as Edmund Sinnott, or a landscape architect such as Ian McHarg with a conservationist such as Aldo Leopold. This group does not deny that life has its many facets—each of them in his special discipline emphasizes that— but the overarching consideration is that all the facets are part of the same diamond. Those mentioned in this book do not make up the whole group, but they do represent a good cross-section of those with an inclusionist mentality. Such a mentality is definitely a minority one in this era of the technological domination of Western culture, if not the whole world.

Among the inclusionists is one individual who is worthy of special attention—Loren Eiseley. This man fully shares with the others a consciousness of the web of life as well as all the concomitant aspects of such a consciousness. Beyond this shared view, however, Eiseley has a very special dimension to his awareness. He has in his perception of nature what one famous theologian, Rudolf Otto, called an awareness of the numinous. Viewing nature, he sees not only empirical interrelatedness and he senses not only aesthetic enjoyment, but he also perceives in it and through it the holy, the miraculous—that awesomeness which has marked religious consciousness from the beginning. In his awareness there is a preternatural perception that gives a sanctity to all life, a depth of feeling and insight that is worthy of formal religious attention, especially in a day when so much formal religion has removed itself from such consciousness.

Eiseley, then, is the central figure among the inclusionists, whom I contrast with the second group, the "exclusionists." This latter group has an indeterminate number of people because it is the one informed by the prevailing definition of nature that excludes man from the overall consideration, and marks out a sharp separation between man and nature.

Obviously, to have any kind of manageable study, representatives from this indeterminate number of people must be selected, and I have chosen my representatives for very special reasons. All are modern men, and all are confessed Christians. I chose them primarily because they are religionists and because they have been recognized by many as on the cutting edge of the thinking of the church. As a group they represent well enough the emphasis on the separation of man and environment, thus standing over against the general stress of the inclusionists. By the fact that they have a particular religious orientation in which their exclusionist views take form, they also stand in sharp opposition to the kind of outlook represented by Eiseley, and thus they form the best kind of contrasting group that can be characterized.

The first representative of the exclusionists is Pierre Teilhard de Chardin as he specified his views in *The Phenomenon of Man*. Being both a paleontologist and a Jesuit priest, he offered a fusion of his scientific and religious positions in a presentation of what he viewed as mankind's evolutionary movement toward a point of complete humanization. This point he called Omega, or, on occasion, God—Omega, showing that the terminus is divine. Teilhard is of particular interest because he shares a common scientific orientation with the inclusionists and yet chooses to interpret what he sees in a way categorically different from them. Where they are holistic, or, more specifically, biocentric, he is almost fiercely anthropocentric, man-centered. As he said in the preface to his book: "I have chosen man as the centre, and around him I have tried to establish a coherent order between antecedents and consequents." [1]

With his anthropocentric emphasis Teilhard is in close company with the other two exclusionist representatives I have chosen, theologians Herbert Richardson and Harvey Cox. Richardson, in his book, *Toward an American Theology,* argues that a "wholly artificial environment" is forthcoming under the leadership of American technology; and out of what seems to be a deep concern for relevancy to such an environment and the society that will exist within it, he argues for a new theological orientation. From the exposition he offers I surmise that he sees man not just separated from the natural order, in the usual understanding of separation, but as absolutely dominant over it to the point where it is utterly submerged.

Cox does not go that far, but in speaking of technopolis in *The Secular City* and megalopolis in *On Not Leaving It to the Snake,* he clearly indicates that nature in any untrammeled form will exist in

[1] Pierre Teilhard de Chardin, *The Phenomenon of Man,* trans. by Bernard Wall (New York: Harper, Torchbook Ed., 1965), p. 29.

sparse lots and only because man allows it, and that the major and completely dominant reality of the future will be the city, that most distinct expression of man's separation from nature.[2]

When there are such fundamental differences as exist between the inclusionists and exclusionists, a systematic determination of their relative merit is demanded. This determination I make, using both pertinent theological considerations and relevant scientific data. At stake in this determination are several issues that have emerged in the course of the study of the two contrasting groups.

One very important issue has to do with the proper understanding and application of control. To what degree does and can man control nature, and to what degree is he controlled by it? What are the signs of improper control by man, and what may be the result of it? What theological understanding, if any, can be applied to the control of nature by man or of man by nature? These are the kinds of questions that the previously mentioned determinations are designed to answer.

Another issue has to do with the proper response to the natural order. This will be determined in part

[2] In discussing the exclusionist representatives I am in no way implying that they are ignorant of the fact that man, biologically speaking, is joined with the rest of nature. What I am pointing out is that this fact does not enter any kind of decisive determination of their views.

by the answers forthcoming in connection with the issue of control. But it depends also on the basic question of what the natural order is. Does the truth lie with Eiseley, who views the given environment with wonder and regards it as a channel through which flows the divine reality, or with Cox, who goes to great lengths to show that nature must be "desacralized"? The answer to such a question goes a long way in determining the way men behave toward the natural order, meaning that choosing between the inclusionist and exclusionist positions carries profound ethical implications.

Finally, closely allied to the issues of control and response, is one already alluded to: the issue over the correct perspective on man. The questions to be decided here are the ones implied by the two definitions of nature. Is man to be understood as standing over against or as in the environment? Is the basic stress to be on dependence or independence or, possibly, interdependence? Is man so little lower than the angels that the natural order is to be a secondary consideration at best, or is he of the dust and therefore inextricably tied to the rest of creation?

After coming to a judgment between the two contrasting schools of environmental thought and how they answer the questions posed by the critical issues, there is the need to offer proposals as to how we are to proceed in light of such judgment. This I shall do, not in any definitive sense but specifically enough so as to save the study from being an academic exercise and to offer some direction toward what I feel is the correct man-nature relation.

II Inclusionists

Life scientists from several fields compose the bulk of those who make up the group I call the inclusionists. They view life as a unity—a gestalt—with the whole of life to be understood as greater than the sum of its parts. To use a figure apropos to our age, they view the earth as a self-contained biological spaceship that functions properly only when its many complex and interrelated systems are in correct balance and "complementation." They do not deny the importance of any given system or aspect of life, but they do object to its ultimate consideration in isolation.

For example, Dr. Barry Commoner in his book

Science and Survival comments on the problem of a specialized study such as molecular biology, which tends to lead to a lack of attention toward the larger biological spectrum. "The dominance of the molecular approach in biological research," he says, "fosters inattention to the natural complexity of biological systems." This, he notes, is particularly true of those systems which "cannot be neatly enclosed in a cage and studied in a laboratory—those which constitute the living environment into which all animals, plants, and man must fit or perish." As a result, he concludes that "today we fail to perceive this system as a complex whole." [1]

The noted paleontologist, George Gaylord Simpson, underwrites such a contention, noting that

> there is a hierarchy of complexity that runs from atoms through molecules, cells, tissues, organs, individuals, specific populations, communities and comprehensive ecological systems to the whole realm of the organic and its environments in space and time. . . . Each level of the hierarchy includes that below. *Knowledge of included levels is necessary but is not sufficient for complete understanding of those more inclusive.* (Emphasis added.) [2]

Viewing the whole of biological life in interrelationship, it follows naturally enough that these in-

---

[1] Barry Commoner, *Science and Survival* (New York: Viking Press, 1963), pp. 45-46.

[2] George Gaylord Simpson, "The Crisis in Biology," *The American Scholar*, Summer, 1967, p. 367.

clusionists do not look favorably upon an anthropocentric, i.e., a completely man-centered, view. Man is no isolated being for them, and any emphasis on his isolation is viewed as both inaccurate and dangerous. Ian McHarg, a teaching and practicing landscape architect, offers the reminder that man, biologically speaking, is, "a plant parasite, dependent upon the plant kingdom and its associated microorganisms, insects, birds and animals for all atmospheric oxygen, all food, all fossil fuel, natural fibers and cellulose, for the stability of the water cycle and amelioration of climate and microclimate.[3]

McHarg is a forceful, outspoken, yet witty, critic of man's concentration upon himself and the way he constantly views himself as outside the grasp of nature. Against such an emphasis McHarg claims, "Truly there is in nature no independence. . . . There can be no enduring system occupied by a single organism. The minimum, in a laboratory experiment, requires the presence of at least two complementary organisms. . . . Conceptions of independence and anthropocentrism are baseless."[4]

One result of the awareness of dependence is a

[3] Ian McHarg, "The Place of Nature in the City of Man." Reprint from *The Annals of the American Academy of Political and Social Science*, March, 1964, p. 12.

[4] McHarg, "Man and Environment" (paper prepared for Dept. of Landscape Architecture, University of Pennsylvania, n.d.), pp. 23-24.

reaffirmation of the reality of the balance of nature. Components of the overall life system depend upon one another, and this dependence involves the maintenance of a certain proportion among them. One strong reaffirmation of the balance of nature came from Rachel Carson in her important book, *Silent Spring*. She noted there that the whole idea of balance was seen in many quarters as passé. This point of view she considered as terribly unfortunate, saying that though "the balance of nature is not the same today as in Pleistocene times . . . it is still there: a complex, precise, and highly integrated system of relationships between living things which cannot safely be ignored any more than the law of gravity can be defied with impunity by a man perched on the edge of a cliff." [5]

Her mention of the change from the Pleistocene Age points to the reason that the idea of the balance of nature is not as central in many areas of thought and action as it once was. This idea understands the balance of nature as some sort of static, once-for-all condition that denies the reality of alteration. However, this is not what the inclusionists think of as the balance of nature. As Miss Carson put it: "The balance of nature is not a status quo, it is fluid, ever shifting, in a constant state of ad-

[5] Rachel Carson, *Silent Spring* (New York: Fawcett Crest Books, 1964), p. 218.

justment.''[6] The balance is a matter not of fixed but of dynamic equilibrium. It operates within sometimes large margins of alteration, but the extent and magnitude of the margins do not eliminate the reality of limits which, if exceeded, mark an imbalance. Thus any given plant or animal species may greatly flourish in one year or season and be greatly diminished in another one; however, the fact that this occurs does not obviate the reality of limits, meaning that if the species becomes too large or is reduced to too few numbers, disaster attends it. And this, very significantly, applies to man as to every other species.

This concept of a dynamic equilibrium defining the balance of nature stems from the commanding discipline of the inclusionists. That discipline is ecology, from the Greek word ''oikos,'' meaning house. It is the study of the ''house,'' that is, the total structure within which man and other creatures exist and of which they are part—the natural environment.

More formally, it is the study of the relationships of organisms and their environment. On the scale of biological studies— beginning with protoplasm and running up through cells, tissues, organs, organisms, populations, communities, ecosystems, and the biosphere (the latter indicating either a large region of the earth or the whole earth itself)

[6] *Ibid.*

—ecology is mainly concerned with the last four categories. Ecology has been adopted as at least a sub-discipline in many fields; for instance, in sociology there is reference to urban ecology, and in demography there is reference to human ecology.

However, the inclusionists, who look at more than strictly human affairs, insist that to use ecology in this way is to misuse it. The claim is that once the web of life is subdivided and all the factors are not brought into consideration, one is no longer looking at things from an ecological point of view. As an example, they cite how very often "ecological" investigations are made with only human populations considered. This, it is said, is not ecology; it is an investigation using ecological methods, but marred by anthropocentric bias.

Ecology, then, is the study that commands the empirical aspect of the inclusionists' position. Yet it is necessary to point out that the science of ecology is far from that sophisticated level of development which marks such sciences as physics and chemistry, nor does it have the long background of such fields of study as philosophy and theology. The term "oecology" was not used until 1869 (by the German zoologist Haeckel),[7] and now, a century later, it still is in no more than its scientific adolescence. For this reason many of its findings are tentative and in-

[7] Cf. George L. Clark, *Elements of Ecology*, rev. ed. (New York: Wiley, 1966), p. 13.

complete. But the "adolescent" science is gaining more and more attention, and ecology is far from being some exotic discipline yet to enter into the mainstream of scientific and social concern.

How far into the mainstream it has proceeded can be illustrated by reference to a report submitted to the Secretary of Health, Education and Welfare in June, 1967, by a special task force on environmental health. The task force noted that environmental health problems were far too complex to be left to the attention of physicians and engineers alone. They called for consultation with physical scientists, life scientists, and social scientists, all of whom would have an understanding of the complexity of the relationship between man and environment, that is, who would be ecologically oriented.[8] In that same report the task force somewhat obliquely underscored the fact that the inclusionists are representatives of a minority view by noting that "much that is wrong with the environment comes about through lack of attention in our educational process to the subject of man's responsibility as custodian of the world about him."[9]

In spite of its admitted limitations, ecology has progressed far enough to have come to some widely agreed upon generalizations. One of these deals with

[8] Task Force on Environmental Health and Related Problems, *A Strategy for a Livable Environment* (Washington, D.C.: Government Printing Office, 1967), p. 43.

[9] *Ibid.*, p. 29.

27

the concept of dynamic equilibrium, already discussed. [Another generalization holds that the
natural systems of the earth are healthiest when
they are diverse. In connection with this generalization the earlier statements of McHarg will be
recalled. The implication is that all forms of life
are seen as valuable, even though the "functions"
of some may not be completely understood.]

Commenting on diversity, a leading ecologist,
Eugene P. Odum, notes that "it is now generally
assumed . . . that the advantage of a diversity of
species—that is, the survival value of the [ecologi-
cal] community—lies in increased stability. The
more species present, the greater the possibilities
for adaptation to changing conditions." Odum goes
on to apply this to man, saying reliance on just a
few crops in his agricultural ecosystems could lead
to disaster with the advent of any widespread, unexpected change.[10]

Going on to the implication of an emphasis on
diversity, Odum states that "above all, the study
of ecology suggests that we should have a healthy
respect for all forms of life. While the 'good guys'

[10] Eugene P. Odum, *Ecology* (New York: Holt, Rinehart &
Winston, 1963), p. 34. Diversity in agriculture has special relevance today, since in light of its burgeoning population humanity
is seeking to increase food production dramatically; and such
increase seems unlikely unless large stretches of land are given
over to a few grain crops, the staple of the world's human population. Yet to do this would run the exact risk to which Odum
refers.

and the 'bad guys' may be clearly distinguishable on the dramatic stage, such is not the case in real life. Many seemingly useless organisms turn out to be useful." [11] Again, applying this idea of diversity to man, Odum remarks how it is good that the biosphere has such a variety of organisms, since some of them can withstand even the severe pollution to which man has subjected natural systems, and by their presence keep the systems viable. Summing up the point, the ecologist says that, "Until we have scientific evidence to the contrary it is clearly in our interest to preserve . . . the remarkable diversity of taxa that have developed during the evolution of the biosphere over millions of years." [12]

The reference to millions of years is characteristic of ecologists and of the inclusionists as a whole. Their perspective on time is not limited to that comparatively brief period of man's civilization but extends far back to prehuman and protohuman times. With such a perspective the inclusionists have a view concerning change that often clashes with the prevailing modern view. They do not argue the fact of change—to them it is inevitable—but they have serious doubts about the rate of change as it has come to be manifested in modern life.

Again Rachel Carson is an appropriate spokesman. While studying the sometimes disastrous

[11] *Ibid.*, pp. 34-35.
[12] *Ibid.*, p. 35.

effects of applied entomology (the study of insect life) she noted that while it took hundreds of millions of years to produce the life that is now on earth, man in less than a century has acquired significant power to alter the given nature of the world, and has proceeded to do so at an increasing and uninformed rate. As she says, "Given time—time not in years but in millennia—life adjusts, and a balance has been reached." But she continues ruefully that "in the modern world there is no time. . . . The rapidity of change and the speed with which new situations are created follow the impetuous and heedless pace of man rather than the deliberate pace of nature." [13] This perspective on time had special relevance to her study, since she claimed that the proper adjustment on the part of man to the presently deleterious effects of pesticides would take not the lifetime of man, but generations—in other words, time as measured on nature's scale and not on the scale of modern man.

Doubt about man's pace and rate of change is also expressed in connection with humanity's proliferation. Human increase, both in terms of rate and of absolute numbers, has accelerated dramatically, especially over the last three hundred years. This has resulted in unprecedented changes, many of them bad and the majority of them unforeseen. With the increasing rate of change there has been increasing

[13] Carson, *Silent Spring*, p. 17.

disregard for equilibrium and diversity, which ecology has shown to be so important. In this light it is not surprising that the English biologist, W. H. Thorpe, would say, "Modern man . . . considered solely as an animal is just about the nastiest creature that has ever been evolved! He is nasty not primarily through lack of good principles . . . but because of his ignorance and stupidity where he at least has the means to be far-seeking and sensible." [14]

What Thorpe puts in his own rather nasty way is, nevertheless, a common thought among the inclusionists. Man is viewed as a species in the midst of a runaway rate of increase that can result only in calamity—both for himself and for the rest of the biosphere. It follows, then, that the inclusionists consider population control an unquestionable necessity.[15]

In his discussion of the population problem Thorpe touches on the fact that it greatly worsened with the widespread practice of death control, along with

[14] W. H. Thorpe, *Science, Man and Morals* (Ithaca: Cornell University Press, 1966), p. 119.

[15] One aspect of the population question not generally touched upon by those whom I have called inclusionists is the means of population control. However, by the fact that life scientists, especially biologists, tend to define life as beginning with the cell, and because some of them emphasize the individual, one could intelligently guess that they would question the use of abortion, at least on a large scale. Of course, there are biologists who do not hesitate to support abortion. Dr. Paul Ehrlich, for instance, in his book *The Population Bomb*, gives blanket endorsement to it.

a disregard of corresponding birth control, following World War II.[16] This, he says, is an example of a failure to practice what he calls synecology, a coined word meaning the scientific and quantitative study of the entire web of life. So, in connection with population matters he voices the same kind of complaint as did Dr. Commoner in connection with molecular biology.

Complaints such as those coming from Thorpe and Commoner illustrate how the inclusionists, though very often scientists themselves and though fully recognizing the genius and accomplishment of much of science and its application, have a running argument with what they consider the major drift of science and technology. They see physics and chemistry as far advanced; they see space technology and cybernetics being highlighted; they see processes that produce new substances and gadgets given great attention; and with all this they see ecological and environmental studies in a scrambling, secon-

[16] There is really no argument among demographers that death control has been the major impetus behind post-World War II population growth. A representative statement is this one offered by Harold F. Dorn: "The major cause of the recent spurt in population increase is a worldwide decline in mortality. Although the birth rate increased in some countries—for example, the United States—during and after World War II, such increases have not been sufficiently widespread to account for more than a small part of the increase in the total population of the world." From "World Population Growth: An International Dilemma," *The Population Crisis and the Use of World Resources* (Bloomington: Indiana University Press, 1964), p. 52.

dary position. Their complaints might be dismissed as professional jealousy, except for the fact that they insist that a continuation of the imbalance in scientific investigation and technological application will bring about dire repercussions. In a later chapter some of the specific empirical findings that lend support to their claim will be presented.

Right here it should be mentioned that the inclusionists do not consider everything empirically. Another very important focus in their position has to do with the aesthetic dimension of the environment. This aspect, of course, is harder to specify, but such a difficulty does not lessen its reality or importance.

So, for example, Harrison Brown in his book, *The Challenge of Man's Future,* rounds off a long examination of the empirical facts concerning man and his environment by shifting to the other, more intangible area. He calls for a re-establishment of contact with our natural environment, noting that, "The flower and vegetable garden, green grass, the fireplace, the primeval forest with its wondrous assemblage of living things, the uninhabited hilltop where one can silently look at the stars and wonder —all of these things and many others are necessary for the fulfillment of man's psychological and spiritual needs." [17] He admits that such things as these

[17] Harrison Brown, *The Challenge of Man's Future* (New York: Viking Press, Compass Books, 1956), pp. 257-58.

have no "practical value," and they do not seem to have much connection with such pressing items as greater food supply and more living space. He insists, however, that they "feed" the total human being in no less an important way than foodstuffs do.

Brown's thought gains an echo in Dr. Charles Ping of Tusculum College. In an article dealing with what he called the problem of sheer human numbers, Ping noted that in this day of bloated human population much of the discussion centers on adequate space and sufficient food with the implication being that if there are these, there is life. To this proposition he replies: "While it is obviously true that without adequate food and space there can be no life, and with little food and space life is haggard and drawn, the equation does not hold when reversed. Adequate food and space does not equal life." [18] Man does not live by bread alone; somewhere there have to be Brown's uninhabited hilltops and primeval forests.

Still another variation on this theme comes from Lewis Mumford, who for a long time has had doubts about the way man concentrates on the narrow extension of himself in the form of his machine culture. He claims that "post-historic man" will have to be

[18] Charles J. Ping, "Numbers and Quality," Special Background Papers for the Alma College American Assembly on the Population Dilemma, April 6-9, 1967.

careful to eliminate all natural reminders of a richer past if he is to maintain future security and the worship of his god, the machine. However, he feels such elimination will occur, since already, as he says, all natural living spaces are being transformed into "low-grade urban tissue." Mumford feels man might somehow manage to have just enough food and space to survive, but notes that their attainment probably will involve "a uniform type of man . . . in a uniform environment, kept at constant temperature, pressure and humidity, living a uniformly lifeless existence, with his uniform physical needs satisfied by uniform goods . . . all inner waywardness brought into conformity by hypnotics and sedatives, or by surgical extirpations, a creature under constant mechanical pressure from incubator to incinerator." [19] Noting such a creature, Mumford questions why anyone or anything, including a machine, should want to keep such a controlled being alive.

If man does manage to eke out enough food and space for survival, Mumford's prognosis is quite feasible. And it points to a very ironic paradox involving man's control of the earth. As man more and more dominates the earth (with domination seen as one expression of control), he seems to cease to be its master, in another sense of the word control,

[19] Raymond Dassman, *Environmental Conservation* (New York: Wiley, 1959), pp. 292-93, quoting Mumford, "The Transformations of Man," *World Perspectives,* 1956.

to a proportionate degree. For if control is taken to mean the ability to have the kind of life one wants when one wants it, then this is precisely what most men cannot have. In his present condition man has only one prospect: to live in an ever more crowded, manipulated environment.

The inclusionists say such a prospect is nightmarish. They reassert the need for the healing interstices of unmodified nature, as well as for a variety in human life. Just as they affirm the belief that a variety of taxa are needed for biological stability, so, too, they feel that a variety of setting and cirsumstance is needed for psychological stability. Thus they abhor the filling in of the interstices of the environment with the "low-grade urban tissue" to which Mumford refers. They point out that such filling in can be permanent, obviously, as in the case of urban sprawl, or can be manifested by the means of widespread mobility and recreation, especially prominent among Americans, whereby the "open" spaces take on the character of urbanized land even though not urban in the strict sense. Signs of this phenomenon are displayed in superhighways, billboards, drive-ins. Other signs include the roar of jet airplanes overhead and crowded camping sites where people go "to get away from it all."

Though in analysis one can separate the aesthetic from the empirical, and one can talk of the "quality of the environment" on one hand and the proper control of it on the other, the inclusionists point out that actually the empirical and aesthetic are inseparable aspects of the same reality. Thus, as a very ordinary example, when a river is made the dumping area for urban-industrial wastes the inclusionists note that, first of all, if man releases an excessive amount of wastes, he has exercised an improper control over nature, the proof of which lies in the fact that the river's own natural capacity for self-cleansing (its own control capacity) has been exceeded. At the same time that this empirical fact is in evidence, the quality or aesthetic aspect also comes into play. As a river becomes more and more polluted the oxygen content becomes depleted, meaning that wildlife cannot subsist on it and, finally, that fish, except for possibly certain "trash" species, are eliminated from it. Also, the flora along the river's banks may change until finally the river becomes a barren sludge ditch if not an open sewer.

Unless one is prepared to say that a sludge ditch, or even a highly polluted river, is the aesthetic equivalent of a clear water concourse, then it must be admitted that there has been an alteration in quality—an alteration for the worse. So, too, as the dirty water becomes undesirable not only for wildlife and fish, it becomes undesirable for human consumption. Here "quality" takes on empirical overtones as well as retaining aesthetic meanings. Human beings *must have* water that is "quality" water, in the sense of a certain level of biological purity, and they want water that is "quality" water in the sense that it is not cloudy or colored and does not carry an offensive odor.

With both empirical and aesthetic considerations in mind the inclusionists have a vision of the ideal earth which contrasts sharply both with other visions and with the likelihood of what will actually transpire if present trends continue. Harrison Brown's own utopia is where machines function enough to relieve men of boring, atrophying work, but machines are tools always put in a very secondary position. In this world man lives in balance with the environment—the land is treated properly, with erosion and overcropping avoided; wastes are returned to the soil; and population is stabilized. Life is efficient enough, but artificiality is minimized. There is government and organization, but government exists for man and not vice versa. Brown's overall view is one of moderation and balance, though the understanding is that the individual living in a diversified world with "myriads of other life forms, which are beneficial to him" and contrasting cultural forms, will have an opportunity for a veritable infinitude of expression and experience. Brown asks himself the same question that he is sure frenetic modern man will ask: Is such a world impossible of realization? He replies by saying, "Perhaps it is, but . . . at least if we try to create such a world there is a chance that we will succeed." He goes on to say that "if we let the present trend continue it is all too clear that we will lose forever those qualities of mind and spirit which distinguish the human being from the automation."[20]

Another vision, not unlike that of Brown, is offered by Dr. Daniel B. Luten. He writes:

[Let us] suppose that our purpose is a world in which men will not be materially deprived, a world where they can seek out their individual lives, where they can lead lives of dignity. Imagine a diverse world, hot and cold, hard and soft, civilized and wild, naive and sophisticated, proud and humble, competitive as well as cooperative, a world of such variety that the intensification of consciousness can never be dulled for lack of new experience, a world with more things under the sun than any man can know. Consider a world in which black and white can live together but also one in which they can live separately ungrudgingly; where rural life can compete effectively with urban life; where you have, perhaps, societies on asphalt but also societies in grass huts and glad of it; a world in which men can still perceive their genetic heritage of wildness in lands still wild.[21]

From such visions it can be seen that inclusionists are not against cities and civilization. They are

[20] Brown, *The Challenge of Man's Future*, p. 258.
[21] Daniel B. Luten, "How Dense Can People Be?" *Sierra Club Bulletin*, December, 1963.

against having nothing but cities and civilization. They do not argue against man's culture and his dominance in the world. However, they do stand against what they consider are the overly narrow directions of that culture, and what they see as a misunderstanding of dominance.

From these views one also notes what is actually a persistent theme among the inclusionists—an emphasis upon the individual. Now on the basis of sheer semantics it seems incongruous that those with a holistic, an inclusive view, would emphasize the individual. Yet this is precisely what they do. Luten speaks of men seeking out their individual lives; Brown, speaking of the great problem of human values in an age of technics, says, "Here, in truth, we are confronted with the gravest and most difficult of all human problems, for it is one that cannot be solved by mathematics or by machines. . . . Solutions, if they exist, can arise only in the hearts and minds of *individual* men." [22]

To this testimony can be added that of the late botanist, Edmund Sinnott. He reminded his readers that "human beings are not turned out by a process of mass production but every individual, so to speak, is custom made to his own genetic specifications." Sinnott notes that this differentiation is confirmed by such things as the particular set of fingerprints each one carries, marking out each person as unique.

[22] *The Challenge of Man's Future*, p. 257.

So he warned that "the sacredness of the distinctive human *individual* . . . is always in danger of being lost to sight. We are accustomed to dealing with atoms and dollars and votes, all standardized units . . . and are tempted to treat men in the same way." [23]

Thorpe also casts doubt on the "standardized unit" being adopted among men. In speaking about eugenics, he quotes with favor the sentiments of T. Dobzhansky, who said: "The implied assumption that there is or can be *the* ideal human genotype which it would be desirable to bestow upon everybody is not only unappealing but almost certainly wrong—it is human diversity that has acted as a creative leaven in the past and will so act in the future." [24]

Here we begin to get an insight into why the semantic incongruity does not turn out to be a logical one. The inclusionists emphasize the individual precisely for the sake of diversity. The ecological generalization that informs them in regard to complimentary species of plants and animals is maintained in regard to individual human beings. They oppose mass man, since he is inclined to make the human landscape as regulated and monochromatic as a one-crop agricultural ecosystem, and because of

[23] Edmund Sinnott, *The Bridge of Life* (New York: Simon and Schuster, 1966), pp. 130-31.
[24] Quoted by Thorpe, *Science, Man and Morals*, p. 124.

that make it vulnerable to disaster through an inability to adjust. They also oppose mass man on aesthetic grounds, feeling that different kinds of people enliven the existence of each person.

Implicit in this kind of emphasis is the understanding that the type of individual which they would emphasize and defend is the responsible one. They are not so naive as to call all kinds of individualism good, but they feel that an eclipse of the individual is an unquestionable evil.

Individuals are highlighted in the writing of the inclusionists, especially ones who have stood against the majority's view of the environment and man's proper relationship to it. More than one speaks of Francis of Assisi shining like a beacon in the midst of an otherwise dark Christian attitude toward the natural world. They speak of Thoreau, who epitomized the doubt about man and his mechanics, and of John Muir, who popularized the idea of national parks and of wilderness as valuable per se, right at the time when exploitation and lack of foresight concerning natural and resource treasures was at its peak. And Rachel Carson is pointed to by her fellow environmentalists as a very recent example of how one individual disclosed the great danger of a heretofore unknown problem, thus throwing an entire industry into doubt, and in large measure initiating what are now growing ecological investigations.

Here, then, is a cross-section of inclusionists and aspects of their view. They call for an awareness of the environment as an integrated unity, with man seen in symbiotic relationship rather than, in any biological way, being separated. They emphasize balance, though stressing that it is to have a fluctuating, dynamic connotation rather than a fixed, rigïd one. Their empirical view is commanded by the comparatively young and admittedly uneven science of ecology, and such a view determines the tangïble focus in a structure of thought that is balanced by a more intangible aesthetic focus. In reality they would point out that the two focuses fuse.

Their perspective on time is geologïc in proportion, and it leads them to cast doubts on the rate of change now manifested by man, especially in his scientific and technological expressions. They support the control of human population, a view made easier by a lack of anthropocentricism, but at the same time they emphasize the sanctity and importance of the individual. They look forward to a world where man functions as a knowledgeable dominant, showing moderation in his biological and technologïcal activity so as to broaden, deepen, and guarantee the future of his perception and consciousness.

If this were the sum total of what has and could emerge from the inclusionists, it would be important enough. More than this has emerged from their midst, however. There has also come, as I shall specifically illustrate with one individual, an awareness of life that, though tied to the empirical and aesthetic, actually stretches beyond it into the realm of the religious.

III An Eloquent Spokesman

What one finds in connection with other inclusionists one most assuredly finds with Loren Eiseley, anthropologist, naturalist, teacher, observer.

Preeminently Eiseley is an evolutionist, meaning that he sees emergent man within a very wide time perspective. He observes the many changes that have occurred across that spectrum of time and how they have accelerated in the last few centuries because of man's great activity. His comment on the acceleration is not typical of those in Western society. He says that though the great specilization of gray matter in the human being has opened up the climates of the world, given us poetry and music, and given at least some people great material holdings and luxury, this specialized matter of the brain has proved to have one terrible flaw: it is too adaptable. As he puts it: "In venturing free of instinct and venturing naked into a universe which demands constant trial and experiment, a world whose possibilities were unexplored and unlimited, man's hunger for experience became unlimited also. He has the capacity to veer with every wind." [1]

This over-adaptability has led man to believe that he has somehow released himself from the regulated channel of time. The argument is that biological evolution has given way to cultural evolution and that man, the culmination of the former,[2] is complete master of the latter. Man is no longer determined by the heartbeat of evolutionary life. In one sense Eiseley does not argue with this, although he reminds modern man that time has a setting and location, and that alteration and accelerated pace must come to grips with the physical environment within whose context they are manifested. He acknowledges that with man came a new penetration

[1] Loren Eiseley, "Man: The Lethal Factor," *American Scientist*, 1963, pp. 71-83.

[2] Eiseley takes exception to the claim that biological evolution has come to a halt. He notes that today there are some species of fish that crawl onto tidal flats in pursuit of insects, that sleep in grass by ponds, and that drown as a man would if held underwater too long. All these are telltale signs of adaptation from aquatic to terrestrial life. The mudskipper *Periophthalmus* has adapted to the point where it climbs trees in pursuit of insects and eats worms like a robin. Cf. *The Immense Journey* (New York: Random House, 1957), p. 58.

of life in the realm of mind, "the realm in which things could be created which could not be brought out of the natural universe itself." Yet he notices that it is the natural universe which after all has created this realm.

Thus he warns that man must never forget from whence he came and of what he still is very much a part. "If we get too remote," he says, "from the world out of which we came—too remote from green leaves, too remote from waters, ancestral waters in the sense that we still carry [them] in our living bodies—there is a danger that in the mechanical constructions which the mind itself can create that we may forget that we exist and live by this world out of which we have emerged." [3]

Eiseley elaborates on this and relates it specifically to the contemporary era this way:

One might say that all organisms that run loose, that escape for the moment out of the living web that controls them, have this potential danger within them. If one flies over any extended area of the country I think that one can almost see this as one might look at fungus spreading on an orange. Because one sees these great urban concentrations of people spreading and spreading, the forest disappearing, the concrete highways extending farther and farther, and although in a sense, and momentarily perhaps, it represents the spread of civilization,

[3] Statement from a transcript of the television program, "The House We Live In," WCAU-TV, Philadelphia, February 5, 1961.

along with it goes this danger of overpopulation, this divorce once again from the nature that we are far more dependent [upon] than we realize.[4]

Eiseley promises that the divorce will have its repercussions. He says man is part of the living web that runs from microorganisms through human beings, and greatly altering the web or breaking through it will only result in nature striking back at the overly adventurous emergent—man.

As with the other inclusionists, Eiseley's awareness of the web of life forms a biocentric view that eliminates the possibility of concentrating exclusively on man. To him man is a wonder, but man is not the only wonder or possibly even the last one. He says,

In many a fin and reptile foot I have seen myself passing by—some part of myself, that is, some part that lies unrealized in the momentary shape I inhabit. People have written me harsh letters and castigated me for a lack of faith in man when I have ventured to speak of this matter in print. . . . They would bring God into the compass of a shopkeeper's understanding and confine Him to those limits, lest He proceed to some unimaginable and shocking act—create, perhaps as a casual afterthought, a being more beautiful than man. As for me, I believe nature capable of this, and . . . I feel no envy—any more than the frog envies the reptile or an ancestral ape should envy man.[5]

[4] *Ibid.*
[5] Eiseley, *The Immense Journey*, pp. 24-25.

In Eiseley's view the trouble stems from what he calls man's continuing Ptolemaic vision. Man sees himself as the center around which everything else does or should revolve. If man were to cease to be, it is felt that the sun would go out and the earth blacken. Everything that lives apart from man is seen as having only a contingent worth, dependent on what it can be or do for men. Against this, he sees the value of life, in whatever form, as intrinsic.

Although Eiseley is not man-centered, he is also not a misanthrope, a hater of man. He notices that man has evolved from many other forms and has been given that profound, differentiating organ, the brain. Man is mentally—though, very importantly, not biologically—unique. This uniqueness, kept in the proper ecological context, must be treasured and cultivated. Like his fellow inclusionists he feels the emphasis of such cultivation must be on man, the individual.

By the very fact that each man has a brain, each man is unique. A man is not so important because he is the representative of the species *Homo sapiens,* a circumstance whereby he could be considered some kind of replaceable part in the mechanism of mankind; rather, man is to be seen as important precisely because it is *he* who *is*. Therefore he says, "The individual must be re-created in the light of a revivified humanism which sets the value of man, the unique, against the vast and ominous shadow of man the composite, the predictable, which is the delight of the machine."[6]

Individuation, then, looms large in Eiseley's view. Reflecting on his own experiences as an ofttimes solitary youth on the Nebraska plain and then as a searching archaeologist in the "waste" areas of the earth, he claims that "sometimes the rare, the beautiful can only emerge and survive in isolation. In a similar manner, some degree of withdrawal serves to nurture man's creative powers."[7] So there must be large interstices, untouched areas in life, where the individual can have the room to nurture his creative powers, where he can have the opportunity to realize that which can be perceived only in isolation and in order that the natural order (without man) which stimulates that perception may flourish and continue to be an inspiration.

Thus it is the perceptive individual in the midst of a world not overly crowded and not overly modified who is seen as important and to whom come insights denied to those in a less favorable milieu. Therefore it is not surprising that Eiseley should write:

It has been said by a great scientific historian that the day of the literary naturalist is done, that the precision of the laboratory is more and more encroaching upon

[6] Eiseley, *Francis Bacon and the Modern Dilemma* (Lincoln: University of Nebraska Press, 1962), p. 80.
[7] Eiseley, *The Mind as Nature* (New York: Harper and Row, 1962), p. 29.

the individual domain. I am convinced that this is a
mistaken judgment. We forget . . . that there is a natural
history of souls, nay, even of man himself, which can be
learned only from the symbolism inherent in the world
about him.

It is the natural history that led Hudson to glimpse
eternity in some old men's faces at Land's End, that led
Thoreau to see human civilizations as toadstools sprung
up in the night by solitary roads, or which provoked
Melville to experience in the sight of a sperm whale some
colossal alien existence without which man himself would
be incomplete.

"There is no Excellent Beauty that hath not some
strangeness in the Proportion" wrote [Francis] Bacon
in days of insight. Anyone who has picked up shells
on a strange beach can confirm his observation. But man,
modern man who has not contemplated his otherness . . .
has not realized the full terror and responsibility of existence.[8]

With such observations Eiseley shades over into
a dimension not realized by all his fellow inclusionists. His perception involves an awareness beyond
the measureable (although that is important) and
beyond that which is merely pleasing to the eye and
other senses. As he puts it: "I . . . want to look at
this natural world both from the empirical point of
view and from one which also takes into account
that sense of awe and marvel which is a part of
man's primitive heritage, and without which man

[8] Eiseley, *Francis Bacon and the Modern Dilemma,* pp. 94-95.

would not be man." He goes on to add: "For many of us the Biblical bush still burns, and there is a deep mystery in the heart of a simple seed." [9]

Eiseley's view is preternatural, i.e., he sees the extraordinary in the ordinary, the uncommon in the common. Mood and setting and circumstance arouse in him an awareness that tells of something that is both strangely familiar and familiarly different. In a term given to us by the theologian Rudolf Otto it can be said that Eiseley has an awareness of the numinous.

In one of the appendixes to his book, *The Idea of the Holy*, Otto cites a passage from John Ruskin which he describes as wholly numinous in character. It has to do with the natural order and reads like something out of Eiseley. Speaking of the perception of his youth, Ruskin said:

There was a continual perception of Sanctity in the whole of nature, from the slightest thing to the vastest; an instinctive awe, mixed with delight; an indefinable thrill, such as we sometimes imagine to indicate the presence of a disembodied spirit. I could only feel this perfectly when I was alone; and then it would often make me shiver from head to foot with the joy and fear of it, when after being some time away from hills I first got to the shore of a mountain river, . . . or when I first saw

[9] Eiseley, *The Firmament of Time* (New York: Atheneum, 1967), p. 8.

the swell of distant land against the sunset, or the first low broken wall, covered with mountain moss. . . . The joy in nature seemed to me to come of a sort of heart-hunger, satisfied with the presence of a Great and Holy Spirit. . . . (*Modern Painters,* Popular Edition (George Allen), vol. iii, p. 309.) [10]

Such a passage is like those offered by Eiseley. Indeed the literature of the scientist is laced with them. For the sake of illustration I shall quote one such passage in its entirety to give the full flavor of Eiseley's numinous experience. The following account comes from a time when the scientist was on an archaeological expedition in the badlands of the American West:

It was a late hour on a cold wind-bitten autumn day when I climbed a great hill spined like a dinosaur's back and tried to take my bearings. The tumbled waste fell away in waves in all directions. Blue air was darkening into purple along the bases of the hills. I shifted my knapsack, heavy with the petrified bones of long-vanished creatures, and studied my compass. I wanted to be out of there by nightfall, and already the sun was going sullenly down in the west.

It was then that I saw the flight coming on. It was moving like a little close-knit body of black specks that danced and darted and closed again. It was pouring from the north and heading toward me with the undeviating relentlessness of a compass needle. It streamed through

[10] Quoted by Otto, *The Idea of the Holy,* trans. John W. Harvey (New York: Oxford University Press, 1958), p. 215.

the shadows rising out of monstrous gorges. It rushed over towering pinnacles in the red light of the sun, or momentarily sank from sight within their shade. Across that desert of eroding clay and wind-worn stone they came with a faint wild twittering that filled all the air about me as those tiny living bullets hurtled past into the night.

It may not strike you as a marvel. It would not, perhaps, unless you stood in the middle of a dead world at sunset, but that was where I stood. Fifty million years lay under my feet, fifty million years of bellowing monsters moving in a green world now gone so utterly that its very light was travelling on the farther edge of space. The chemicals of all that vanished age lay about me in the ground. Around me still lay the shearing molars of dead titanotheres, the delicate sabers of soft-stepping cats, the hollow sockets that had held the eyes of many a strange, outmoded beast. Those eyes had looked out upon a world as real as ours; dark, savage brains had roamed and roared their challenges into the steaming night.

Now they were still there, or, put it as you will, the chemicals that made them were here about me in the ground. The carbon that had driven them ran blackly in the eroding stone. The stain of iron was in the clays. The iron did not remember the blood it had once moved within, the phosphorus had forgot the savage brain. The little individual moment had ebbed from all those strange combinations of chemicals as it would ebb from our living bodies into the sinks and runnels of oncoming time.

I had lifted up a fistful of that ground. I held it

while that wild flight of south-bound warblers hurtled over me into the oncoming dark. There went phosphorus, there went iron, there went carbon, there beat the calcium in those hurrying wings. Alone on a dead planet I watched that incredible miracle speeding past. It ran by some true compass over field and waste land. It cried its individual ecstasies into the air until the gullies rang. It swerved like a single body, it knew itself and, lonely, it bunched close in the racing darkness, its individual entities feeling about them the rising night. And so, crying to each other their identity, they passed away out of my view.

I dropped my fistful of earth. I heard it roll inanimate back into the gully at the base of the hill: iron, carbon, the chemicals of life. Like men from those wild tribes who had hunted these hills before me seeking visions, I made my sign to the great darkness. It was not a mocking sign, and I was not mocked. As I walked into my camp late that night, one man, rousing from his blankets beside the fire, asked sleepily, ''What did you see?''

''I think a miracle,'' I said softly, but I said it to myself.[11]

For this scientist the world is an arena of miracles. Indeed, the natural world in its entirety is a miracle. ''We forget, '' he says, ''that nature itself is one vast miracle transcending the reality of night and nothingness.'' And he goes on to add, significantly: ''We forget that each one of us in his personal

[11] *The Immense Journey,* pp. 170-73.

life repeats that miracle."[12] So it is that man is truly wondrous, but that is only because he is an expression of an order that in its entirety is wondrous. Moreover, the presence of the wondrous world implies the reality of a wonder-worker. "I would say," offers Eiseley, "that if 'dead' matter has reared up this curious landscape of fiddling crickets, song sparrows, and wondering men, it must be plain even to the most devoted materialist that the matter of which he speaks contains amazing, if not dreadful powers, and may not impossibly be, as Hardy has suggested, 'but one mask of many worn by the Great Face behind.' "[13]

Eiseley is a living datum supporting the thesis of Otto, and he is a very important one since he is a learned scientist with his credentials fully in order and his renown rather widespread. He embodies and can give very eloquent expression to a consciousness that could be dismissed only if he were judged mentally unbalanced. But most of his critics have come away feeling that his consciousness has made modern man appear mentally deprived.

Eiseley is not alone in his awareness of awe and wonder. It was underwritten, for instance, by his fellow inclusionist, Edmund Sinnott, who said:

The greatest mysteries are ones we know exist but seem beyond the power of intellect alone to resolve—

[12] *The Firmament of Time,* p. 171.
[13] *The Immense Journey,* p. 210.

the origin and destiny of the universe, the nature of space and time, the character of life and its relation to matter and to man, and the dependence of mind and matter on each other. Before these, an attitude of wonder and reverence, so out of fashion in these days of certainty, can hardly be avoided.[14]

Other supporting statements and examples could be cited from other scientists,[15] who, it may be argued, are stirred as were many of their intellectual forebears by the very wonder of it all. I have chosen to focus on Eiseley only because the experiences of his awareness are so dramatic and specific. Not only in general but in very particular instances he can signify the great moral value of the natural order, and note how it stirs religious consciousness.

With such drama in his life Eiseley joins his fellow inclusionists in having doubts about the way science and technology are proceeding. However, in his case it is not simply a matter of scientific imbalance or a lack of Thorpe's synecology; with him it is the reduction of a miracle to the mundane. Or as he tends to put it, it is the tendency to make nature, including man, natural. When nature be-

---

[14] Sinnott, *The Bridge of Life*, p. 216.

[15] One other example comes by the way of Rachel Carson as she quotes C. J. Briejer, director of the Dutch Plant Protection Service. Dr. Briejer claimed, ''We need a more high-minded orientation and a deeper insight, which I miss in many [scientific] researchers. Life is a miracle beyond our comprehension, and we should reverence it even where we have to struggle against it.'' From *Silent Spring*, p. 243.

comes natural it becomes a tool, a device; in the
most popular American expression it becomes "natural resources." In a similar way, man upon becoming natural is reduced more and more to thinghood
and a device to manipulate and "properly control."
Sometimes the problem is sensed generally and
gains expression, as in the American teen-age slo-
gan: "We are human beings. Do not fold, spindle,
or mutilate."

The scientist's own comment on this goes this
way:

Man, in the words of one astute biologist, is "caught
in a physiological trap and faced with the problem of
escaping from his own ingenuity." Pascal, with intuitive
sensitivity, saw this at the very dawn of the modern
era in science. "There is nothing which we cannot make
natural," he wrote, and then, prophetically, comes the
full weight of his judgment upon man, "there is nothing
natural which we do not destroy." *Homo faber,* the tool-
maker, is not enough. There must be another road and
another kind of man lurking in the mind of this odd
creature, but whether the attraction of that path is as
strong as the age-old primate addiction to taking things
apart remains to be seen.[16]

Eiseley is no primitive who wants to burn books
or dismantle all the machinery. Nevertheless he does
say that the brain-carrying primate who, quite sig-

[16] *The Firmament of Time,* p. 159.

nificantly, still carries the jungle instincts within him as well as the accretions of his cultural evolution, is headed for disaster if he merely extends himself along mechanical and technological lines. Man in his "outward" expression runs away from the real problem of man—himself. In his technological preoccupations he continues to delay the time when he finally has to grow up. So, hearkening to another of his intellectual mentors, Eiseley offers this:

"Man is the dwarf of himself," Emerson once wrote, and never perhaps, has he been more the dwarf than in this age where he appears to wield so much power. The only sign of health remaining to him is the fact that he is still capable of creeping out of the interior of his thickening crust of technological accomplishment to gaze around him with a sense of dissatisfaction and unease.

He has every reason to feel this way. For man has never lived in so great an age of exterior accomplishment, so tremendous a projection of himself into his machine, nor yet so disheartening a period in all that stands for the nobler aspects of the human dream. His spiritual yearnings to transcend his own evil qualities are dimming. . . . His desire to fly away to Mars, still warring, still haunted by his own black shadow, is the adolescent escape mechanism of a creature who would prefer to infect the outer planets with his problems than to master them at home.[17]

[17] Eiseley, "An Evolutionist Looks at Modern Man," *Saturday Evening Post*, April 26, 1958, p. 121.

The problem, once again, is that man and nature have become natural. Man, who can and has sensed other dimensions, who has seen in nature the immanence of the One who created it, who has sensed in himself the *imago Dei,* now increasingly is one-dimensional. Progress is not defined almost solely in terms of the attainment of the next invention. In the realm of the spirit, opened up to man once his brain was developed, one notices attenuation and atrophy in the modern, mechanical era. Where in the past (however confusedly) the natural order brought at least some to an awareness of something transcendent, mysterious, and prior, it now is for most, seemingly, either the machine that grinds out its orderly but accidental existence or the mere stage and setting where all-encompassing man can play out the only drama there is.

On the other hand, man, who in his own internal being has sensed something Other, now is so bombarded with stimuli from the outside, both in the form of masses of men and masses of machines and gadgets, that the internal awareness grows weak and the still small voice becomes dumb. With the voice mute, men then begin to feel that the external stimuli are the only realities, so that men and their machines become the measure of all things. Man may still dream, but his dreams can follow along the line of the one dimension alone.

At the conclusion of one of his books, returning

again to Pascal, Eiseley summarizes the problem,
and at the same time offers in tantalizing brevity the
suggestion of the one who may alter man's present
course and lead him to new dimensions and that
"other road." He says,

Man, at last, is face to face with himself in natural
guise. "What we make natural, we destroy," said Pascal. He knew, with superlative insight, man's complete
necessity to transcend the worldly image that this word
connotes. It is not the outward powers of man the toolmak-
er that threaten us. It is a growing danger which has already affected vast areas of the world—the danger that we
have created an unbearable last idol for our worship. That
idol, that uncreate and ruined visage which confronts
us daily, is not less than man made natural. Beyond this
replica of ourselves, this countenance already grown so
distantly inhuman that it terrifies us, still beckons the
lonely figure of man's dreams. It is a nature, not of this
age, but of the becoming—the light once glimpsed by a
creature just over the threshold from a beast, a despairing
cry from the dark shadow of a cross on Golgotha long ago.

Perhaps [even now] there may come to us . . . a ghostly
sense that an invisible doorway has been opened—a doorway which, widening out, will take man beyond the nature
that he knows.[18]

[18] *The Firmament of Time,* pp. 180-81.

IV Exclusionists

Having drawn a profile of those who would include man in the definition of nature, I now turn to those who present views that emphasize a sharp separation of man from his environment. Intellectually, those in this group know that man is part of nature, and yet this fact has no decisive effect upon their writings. They know man is part of nature, but they treat him as though he were not.

As mentioned in the Introduction, three representatives make up this group, with this trio acting as spokesmen for that much larger group which would generally exclude man from a "working" defi-

nition of nature. Two of the representatives have
the Christian faith specifically in the foreground of
their thought, while the third has it in the background of his musings.

I have chosen them because they all have taken
what are considered venturesome steps and thus
may be viewed as imaginative thinkers on the frontier of Christian thought. In one sense they may
be considered a kind of Christian spearhead that
strikes sharply against such a position as I have
outlined as representing the inclusionists, meaning
that they not only present views that emphasize anthropocentrism as against biocentrism, technics and
urbanization as against ecological emphases, but also
religious views that would obviate the numinous
consciousness and its concomitant religious awareness such as we have noted in Loren Eiseley.

The first of these exclusionist representatives is
Pierre Teilhard de Chardin, as he presented his
position in *The Phenomenon of Man*. His is a most
grandiose view, for he looks at man from that time
even before *Homo sapiens* was a biologically finished
form to what he sees as the culmination of man's
earthly existence in the future, a future even more
removed from the present than is man's beginning.
His presentation is supposed to be scientifically de-
tached, but one sees in it the scientific and theological fusion of a man who held the positions of paleontologist and Jesuit priest in his own life. It is true

that he does not thrust his Christian views into the midst of the discussion, but one can see their influence, even though they are in the background.

By the long sweep of his view it can be seen that he shares a characteristic of Eiseley (and other inclusionists), since he too was an anthropologist and evolutionist. In addition, he has a kind of sense of the web of life, although here there is a very important distinction to be drawn. Where those of an inclusionist frame of mind tend to emphasize the web of life by the way it exhibits interrelated, contemporaneous forms of life, Teilhard places this emphasis upon the linear, the time, aspect. He stresses the emergent out of the web, and pre-eminently the "last" emergent—man.

This last emergent has wrought a sudden (geologically speaking) and fantastic change upon the earth. As Teilhard puts it:

This sudden deluge of cerebralisation, this biological invasion of a new animal type which gradually eliminates or subjects all forms of life that are not human, this irresistible tide of fields and factories, this immense and growing edifice of matter and ideas—all these signs that we look at, for days on end—to proclaim that there has been a change on the earth and a change of planetary magnitude.[1]

So far, the change is, at best, no more than in

[1] Teilhard de Chardin, *The Phenomenon of Man,* p. 183.

an intermediate stage. Man has largely "conquered" the biosphere, but he has as yet not completed a sphere "above" the biosphere, a layer of thought, if you please, which Teilhard calls the noosphere. The noosphere (literally the sphere of the mind) is "a single organised membrane over the earth,"[2] where man with his facilities of travel and communication is in a state of forming "an almost solid mass of hominised substance."[3] This noosphere is possible because the earth is limited, that is, spherical, so that now man has filled the interstices, the gaps, of nature and is subject to the increasing pressure, brought about by ever-growing numbers and inventions, which causes him to "involute" upon himself in an accelerating way. As a result of his involution or "turning in upon oneself," Teilhard optimistically sees man, or future man, the terminus of what is in process at present, turning into a single psychosocial unit, the presence of which will actually represent a new type of organism.

This organism will be the end result of the "hominisation" process, meaning that man will be truly human when there is perfect unity in diversity among humankind. The terminus is called Omega, and sometimes it is linked with God, at which point, again, each person is synthesized with the other in perfect harmony, i.e., in love. At Omega each per-

[2] *Ibid.*, p. 242.
[3] *Ibid.*, p. 240.

son will be free of the "defect" of confusing individuality with personality,[4] so that individuation will not be hindering the collectivization of like, loving minds. Omega lies far in the future—"in all probability, between our modern earth and the ultimate earth, there stretches an immense period, characterised not by a slowing-down but a speeding-up and by the definitive florescence of the forces of evolution along the line of the human shoot"[5]— but man is on his way (that is, he is progressive), and he will progress until Omega brings him to "an ecstasy transcending the dimensions and the framework of the visible universe."[6]

At the last, then, Teilhard, like Eiseley, sees man transcending his present nature, although the form of transcendence is quite different. Where Eiseley sees man transcending himself if he turns to another direction from his present one, Teilhard sees the transcendence coming at the end of the pursuit of the present direction. Eiseley challenges the present trend, Teilhard baptizes it. In moving toward the transcendent stage of Omega, man, to put it bluntly, crunches nature by the means of science and technology. Teilhard puts it more elegantly, saying, "Taken in the full modern sense of the word, science is the twin sister of mankind," for, "the march of humanity . . . develops indubita-

[4] *Ibid.*, p. 263.
[5] *Ibid.*, p. 277.
[6] *Ibid.*, p. 289.

bly in the direction of a conquest of matter put to the service of mind."[7] His view is that all nature longs to be mankind, and the earth realizes its ultimate worth only when the unit, man, comes to full expression. Nature has meaning, seemingly, only in that it finally expresses itself in man. Speaking of the present he says,

At the end of its constructions, biology, if it takes its discoveries to their logical conclusion, finds itself forced to acknowledge the assemblage of thinking beings as the present terminal form of evolution. We find man at the bottom, man at the top, and, above all, man at the centre.[8]

In the future the assemblage will become, as said previously, an organism;[9] man in a unity completely

[7] *Ibid.*, pp. 248-49.   [8] *Ibid.*, p. 281.
[9] The possibility of men becoming an organism has been specifically repudiated by one who in many ways was close to being an inclusionist. Aldous Huxley said: "Biologically speaking, man is a moderately gregarious, not a completely social animal —a creature more like a wolf, let us say, or an elephant, than like a bee or an ant. In their original form human societies bore no resemblance to the hive or the ant heap; they were merely packs. Civilization is, among other things, the process by which primitive packs are transformed into an analogue, crude and mechanical, of the social insects' organic communities. At the present time the pressures of over-population and technological change are accelerating this process. The termitary has come to seem a realizable and even, in some eyes, a desirable goal. Needless to say, the ideal will never in fact be realized. A great gulf separates the social insect from the not too gregarious, big-brained mammal; and even though the mammal should do his best to imitate the insect, the gulf would remain. However hard they try, men cannot create a social organism, they can only create an organization. In the process of trying to create an organ-

unrealized today will then be a reality. Man in his
ingenuity and technological extension[10] will bring
himself into an inseparable mesh where thought will
whirl around the noosphere in full floresence,
brotherhood will have a meaning of complete conjunction between persons, and man at his ultimate
will join with God at Omega. There will be a gigantic mega-synthesis; one will be all, and all one.

The second exclusionist has a far less grandiose
view of synthesis than Teilhard, but because his
view is more specific and pertinent to the present
era, it proves to be more compelling. Theologian
Herbert Richardson, in his book, *Toward an American Theology,* indicates that the synthesis that is

ism they will merely create a totalitarian despotism." *Brave New
World Revisited* (New York: Bantam Books, 1960), p. 22.

[10] It should be noted that near the end of his book Teilhard
inserts a section that in my opinion is a reversal of the theme
of the book as a whole. Where everything prior to p. 283 has
emphasized man's uniqueness and his control of the earth, on
that page he abruptly mentions a projected "harmonious concilia-
tion of what is free with what is planned and totalised." He
mentions the need of a whole series of "geo-sciences," including
geo-demography, as well as "the control of the trek towards un-
populated areas." This kind of emphasis means that he is suddenly talking not about man controlling nature as much as about
man controlling himself. And a control of the trek toward un-
populated areas is a statement in favor of interstices, which
stand in sharp contrast to an "almost solid mass of hominised
substance." I gain the impression that Teilhard, almost as an
afterthought, realizes that the inherent limitations of the earth
have to be dealt with in a way other than simply characterizing
them as forcing the "hominisation" of man. This section is an
anomaly in the book, for its implications cast a shadow over the
emphasis that is given everywhere else.

coming is to be understood in connection with the emerging cybernetic systems.

Through what he calls "sociotechnics," he sees the increasing conjunction of man and machine. The conjunction will not be in the form of man controlling machines, as is the common view, or, somehow, machines controlling men on the same subject-object basis as the other; rather, men and machines will actually control one another on a "continuing cycle of inquiry and feedback." [11] By means of computers the whole society will be accurately predictable and thus subject to rational control. No one will stand outside the system (as a dictator would), but everyone will be both a subject and an object within it.

The results of the man-machine conjunction, Richardson predicts, will be "the creation of a wholly artificial environment." [12] Where before, the technique or art of control of an environment used nature as a pattern, now "an entire society will organize in order to reshape itself and its world in accordance with an imaginative vision of the good life." [13]

Man will be extricated completely from the natural environment, it seems, and Richardson says that in this new circumstance Christianity must bring forth a conception of God that will be relevant to

[11] Herbert Richardson, *Toward an American Theology* (New York: Harper, 1967), p. 18.
[12] *Ibid.*, p. 17.
[13] *Ibid.*

the "denaturalized" sociotechnic man. His suggestion is this: "The God of a sociotechnic intellectus [a contrived term meaning context or framework of meaning] must be reconceived as the unity of the manifold systems of the world." [14] This relevant conception must be brought forth, since the author claims the sociotechnic movement is inevitable.

This transformation is inevitable because the knowledge of the sociotechnics is more powerful than the old arts and sciences of the modern world, and is capable of helping us to deal with critical problems of our age—problems the modern world has generated but has not been able to solve.[15]

Thus Richardson is a determinist,[16] flatly affirming that a cybernetic age will transpire, come what may. His determinism stems from his unquestioning embrace of technology. He pinpoints the love of technology as the central American value-orientation, and he feels, as a result, that America is the location not only for the advance into the cybernetic age but also for the proper theological understanding of such an age.

It follows that if the technological value-orienta-

[14] *Ibid.*, p. 23.

[15] *Ibid.*, p. 20.

[16] Teilhard can well be considered a determinist also. He claimed: *"Man is irreplaceable.* Therefore, however improbable it might seem, *he must reach the goal* [attainment of the organism of mankind], not necessarily, doubtless, but infallibly." *The Phenomenon of Man*, p. 276.

tion is foremost in America, the other value-orientations will occupy a subordinate if not a subservient position. Among those value-orientations which end up in a secondary position are individualism and personal freedom. Richardson notes that although these two are as strong in America as they are any place in the Western world, still the unique characteristic of America is her faith in social technology. "The vision of a wholly artificial environment, man and society restructured by the power of the machine, is the American dream." [17] To this he adds, significantly, the fact that this dream has always been sustained by Christian eschatology.

So this theologian traces a Christian source lying behind the idea of progress and betterment, which in his mind are spelled out solely within a technological framework, a framework that brings optimal rational control, though at the cost of individual freedom. So he says: "Sociotechnics regards the free decisions of individuals as mere *quanta* to be ordered within the system of mass society, 'the compass of rationality itself,' " meaning that, "the pantechnicism which is emerging in our time appears to be destroying the individual person and overthrowing the 'holy ultimates' of the modern world of history." [18] This might be regrettable, it seems, if it were not inevitable.

[17] *Toward an American Theology,* p. 28.
[18] *Ibid.,* pp. 19-20.

With the reduction of the individual and the emergence of the wholly artificial environment it is easy to see how sharply Richardson's predictions stand in opposition to the emphases of the inclusionists. A wholly artificial environment would seemingly exclude, or at best reduce to absolute subservience, all forms of natural life except human life, and even the latter would be sharply curtailed in its individual expression. The result of this is a collective anthropocentrism, when considering created forms of life alone. Richardson himself is ultimately theocentric, God-centered, but he is radically man-centered on the biological plane. With his view, the web of life, as the inclusionists perceive it, has been torn asunder. Man, with absolute control, completely transforms the earth, so that the given systems cease to exist and something wholly artificial takes their place.

With his anthropocentrism and his complete espousal of technology Richardson has strong affinity with the thought of Teilhard, although he does not place his presentation in the context of eons as did the paleontologist. Like Teilhard (and thus contrary to the inclusionists) he basically supports present trends, not so much because they are inherently better but because they are so powerful, according to him, that it is useless to resist them. The natural order shall be completely altered, and with it any consciousness that a man like Eiseley might exhibit.

Richardson's fellow theologian, Harvey Cox, does not speak of a wholly artificial environment, but he does predict a situation that approximates that very thing. The natural order will be subjugated as man's separation from it in the form of the city becomes the dominant fact of life. "Future historians will record the twentieth century," he says, "as that century in which the whole world became one immense city." [19] He elaborates by noting that "whereas [cities] once formed mere islands in a vast sea of uncharted nature, today the balance is reversing itself. The world is becoming one huge interdependent city, in which jungles and deserts remain only with the explicit consent of a global metropolis." [20] In one way of looking at it, Cox's world city could be considered the analogue of Teilhard's "single organised membrane over the earth." Looking at the prospect of planetary urbanization Cox's reaction is recorded when he says, "It is thrilling to live in the age of the new world city." [21]

Yet the thrill does not reduce his awareness of many of the problems the urban spread involves. Megalopolis, as he calls it in *On Not Leaving It to the Snake,* or technopolis, as he called it in his earlier book, *The Secular City,* is fraught with problems of

[19] Harvey Cox, *On Not Leaving It to the Snake* (New York: Macmillan, 1967), p. 101.
[20] *Ibid.,* p. 102.
[21] *Ibid.*

poverty, racial strife, a need for new church organization, and many related problems, all of which may be summarized as the challenge of unprecedented power and the control over it that its presence implies. His answer to the challenge is always the same: man must act with imaginative, mature responsibility.

The elements of this responsibility include: (1) an awareness of the autonomy of man brought about by the desacralization of nature, along with the proper perception of God as a liberating partner who frees men to run the world; (2) full adoption of the pragmatic approach to those problems which arise in the technopolitan culture, with an emphasis on solving problems rather than understanding life.

If we take a look at the first of these elements, we find that Cox leans heavily on one of the two accounts of creation in Genesis (the so-called Yahwistic account), claiming that the "Hebrew view of Creation . . . separates nature from God and distinguishes man from nature." [22] The result of this is that "man becomes in effect a subject facing nature. He can still enjoy it and delight in it, perhaps even more so since its terrors have been reduced for him. But man is not a mere expression of nature and nature is not a divine entity." [23] Moreover, relying on this one account of creation, plus a single

---

[22] Cox, *The Secular City* (New York: Macmillan, 1965), p. 22.
[23] *Ibid.*, p. 24.

verse out of the other account of creation (Genesis 1:28), the famous "dominion" verse, Cox claims that "God does not simply insert man into a world filled with creatures which are already named, in relationships and meaning patterns already established by decree. Man must fashion them himself. He simply doesn't discover meaning; he originates it." [24]

The implications of this are clear enough. Man stands over against nature in a subject-object relationship, and the object (nature) is liable to what man decides for it. In Eiseley's terms, this would be one expression (or justification) of making nature natural. Acceptance of this view means that nature is not miraculous and by implication cannot, or somehow should not, lead to an awareness of the numinous. Nature becomes whatever man decides it will be, since he has removed its mystery and tapped the knowledge of its own processes as well as the ones that subdue it.

Cox admits that at times there has been a problem with desacralization. He says: "It is true . . . that modern man's attitude toward disenchanted nature has sometimes shown elements of vindictiveness. Like a child suddenly released from potential restraints, he takes savage pride in smashing nature and brutalizing it." However, he softens the impact of this statement by claiming that "this is

[24] *Ibid.*, p. 74.

perhaps a kind of revenge pressed by a former prisoner against his captor, but it is essentially childish
and is unquestionably a passing phase.''[25]

After emphasizing man's separation from nature
Cox moves to the structure of the God-man partnership. This time, relying on Karl Barth's theology
(which itself strongly emphasizes the man-nature
separation[26]), Cox argues that Barth's ''Wholly
Other'' God is ''a God who doesn't need man, therefore He can let man live. Only when God and man
have been fully differentiated from one another can
God come near to man without limiting and oppressing him.'' Thus, ''as the last stages of myth and
ontology disappear, which they do in Barth's theology, man's freedom to master and shape, to create
and explore now reaches out to the ends of the
earth and beyond.''[27]

Cox, then, like Richardson, is ultimately God-
centered, but in the created order strongly man-
centered. ''Barth's theology,'' he says approvingly,
''supplies the basis for a sweeping kind of Christian
humanism. The whole world, the place where man
is set, is *for* him. It is man's world, not in an abstract or vacuous way, but through divine inten-

[25] *Ibid.*, p. 23.

[26] An exposition of this is given in H. Paul Santmire's ''Creation and Nature: A Study of the Doctrine of Nature with Special
Attention to Karl Barth's Doctrine of Creation'' (unpublished
Th.D. thesis, Harvard, 1966).

[27] *Ibid.*, p. 82.

tionality.'' [28] However, unlike Richardson (and Teilhard) he excludes any kind of determinism. For him the future is ''wide-open,'' and what transpires in it is strictly up to man. Speaking of what he calls prophecy, he says, ''Prophecy produces both the terror and the joy inherent in the recognition that the future will be what man will make of it. . . . This raises the stakes of politics. It makes both heaven and hell a possibility again.'' [29]

The second main element of Cox's view of responsibility offers the ''proper'' means of dealing with this wide open future. That means turns out to be pragmatism, doing what will ''work.'' Cox feels that modern pragmatism must be understood and appreciated. He explains it this way:

To say that technopolitan man is pragmatic means that he is a kind of a modern ascetic. He disciplines himself to give up certain things. He approaches problems by isolating them from irrelevant considerations, by bringing to bear the knowledge of different specialists, and by getting ready to grapple with a new series of problems when these have been provisionally solved. Life for him is a set of problems, not an unfathomable mystery. He brackets off the things that cannot be dealt with and deals with those that can.[30]

[28] *On Not Leaving It to the Snake*, p. 120.
[29] *Ibid.*, p. 44.
[30] *The Secular City*, p. 63.

The author recognizes that pragmatism can become too narrow, becoming what he calls "operationalism," thus wholly excluding an awareness of other aspects of the phenomenon under consideration.[31] By and large, however, he looks approvingly upon this way of dealing with life, feeling that it is a life style to which Christianity can and must be relevant.

Here can be seen one last great contrast between this exclusionist and the inclusionists. The "compartmentalization" of pragmatism is the categorical opposite of the holistic, inclusive emphasis that the various life scientists discussed stand for. It is the very segmentation of life without the desire or effort to see or appreciate its unity which is a central point of contention for those who see life as a web and not like separate folders in a file drawer.

More generally, we can now summarize the broad contrasts that have clearly emerged as we have examined the inclusionist and exclusionist schools of thought. First and foremost, obviously, is the fact that the exclusionists concentrate on man and make him the measure of all creation. Even the theologians who ultimately focus on God present God as a "support datum" for the activity and centrality of man. Over against this the inclusionists refuse to make man such a single center of attention. They

[31] *Ibid.*, p. 67.

do not demean man and his activity; they simply say that an over-concentration on humanity ignores the importance of life in its full variety and, paradoxically, ultimately works against the welfare of man.

The concentration on man leads the exclusionists to underwrite present trends and activities in society, the most active of which are increased technology and urbanization. This is not surprising. It would be incongruous for them to be man-centered and yet be doubtful, let alone condemnatory, of the major contemporary expressions of man. In contrast, the inclusionists do not hesitate to express grave doubts about man's present thrusts. Their allegiance is to life in general, not just one aspect of it, so if one aspect seems to be threatening the overall pattern they do not refrain from speaking out.

The main item that bothers the inclusionists is that man's present direction is toward an ever greater expression of control, which, to their way of thinking, is utterly imperialistic. Indeed, they might call it despotism, and would hold that this despotism, as all others in history, will finally come to a sorry end. On the other hand, the exclusionists would dismiss such a characterization of man's control. What man is doing is not a violation of anything in their eyes; rather, it is what man can rightfully or must inevitably be about. Again their anthropocentrism determines their view. How can man be in violation

79

of something when he is the center of created value?

Such marked contrast of view between the two groups that I have characterized demands some kind of judgment and determination. The gulf between the two general positions is too great to be spanned by some bridge of compromise. One must stand on one side or the other. So the task at hand is to make the determination on the basis of truly pertinent considerations. This I am going to do in the next two chapters.

The first of these will deal with biblical and theological considerations, pertinent because our exclusionists are religionists and because the most profound of the inclusionists, Loren Eiseley, reveals a deep religious consciousness. The second chapter will deal with demographic and ecological considerations, that is, the pertinent empirical data. These data, I contend, are more important than, say, social, economic, and political data (though all these, of course, are related to the physical facts), simply because social institutions, economic structures, and political forms exist only if the physical conditions are favorable enough to allow them. Thus the determination will be made on the basis of religious and scientific judgments.

V Determinations: Biblical and Theological

The determinations between the two contrasting groups begin with a series of biblical and theological considerations. This area is the home territory of the exclusionists (though admittedly Teilhard was as much at home in a strictly scientific context as in a religious one).

Probably the most obvious place to begin the determination is with the doctrine of creation as it is included in the creation myths of Genesis. As was noted, Cox places special reliance upon this doctrine in order to justify his position of the desacralization of nature, and I would contend that what is explicit in Cox is implicit in Richardson as he speaks of the wholly artificial environment, and Teilhard as he speaks of the "thinking layer," or noosphere, which transcends the biosphere, the natural systems layer. More than that, I would say that the interpretation of the doctrine of creation which Cox gives is the latest reaffirmation of what has been the dominant Christian interpretation throughout the centuries.

Certainly there is no doubt in the minds of the inclusionists that this is true. Ian McHarg, for instance, says, "The first chapter of Genesis contains the ruling concept of God, nature and man held by Jews and Christians alike, man made in the image of God, given dominion over all life, enjoined to subdue the earth. It is from this source that Jews and Christians derive the concept of a man-oriented universe; the sense of the earth existing for the delection and use of man, his relation to nature as one of domination and subjugation." [1]

His position gains support from Lynn White, Jr., a historian who has concern for man's relationship with nature. White notes that Christianity inherited from Judaism not only a linear, nonrepetitive concept of time, but also a striking story of creation wherein God created all the various life forms, culminating his work in man. Man was given dominion

[1] McHarg, "Man and Environment," p. 12.

and made unique, so that "no item in the physical creation had any purpose save to serve man's purposes. And although man's body is made of clay, he is simply not part of nature: he is made in God's image." As a result of this White goes on to conclude that,

especially in the Western form, Christianity is the most anthropocentric religion the world has seen. As early as the 2nd century both Tertullian and Saint Irenaeus of Lyon were insisting that when God shaped Adam he was foreshadowing the image of the incarnate Christ, the Second Adam. Man shares, in great measure, God's transcendence of nature. Christianity, in absolute contrast to ancient paganism and Asia's religion (except, perhaps, Zoroastrianism), not only established a dualism of man and nature, but also insisted that it is God's will that man exploit nature for his proper ends.[2]

Here, then, is the source of the anthropocentrism of the exclusionists as well as their explicit working definition of nature as that which stands over against and apart from man.

On the basis of such testimony it would appear that the creation narratives are a complete source of support for the man-centered position. However, such influential material requires direct examination. Looking at them directly, we note, of course, that

[2] Lynn White, Jr., "The Historical Roots of Our Ecologic Crisis," *Science*, March 10, 1967, p. 1205.

there are two creation narratives—the later, priestly account (designated by P) covering Genesis 1 and the first three verses of Genesis 2, and the earlier, Yahwistic account (from the Hebrew name for God, Yahweh, and designated by J) which begins at Genesis 2:4 and runs through the third chapter.

Taking the second account first, we notice that its predominant theme is, beyond all doubt, man; it tells of his creation and fall. The order of creation in this account is as follows: man, vegetation, animals, and, finally, woman. Being first, man has "priority rights," as it were. Man's predominance is further enhanced by the fact that in this account it is said that God brought all the beasts and birds to man who, in turn, named them (Genesis 2:19). Naming was perceived as virtually a creative activity in Hebrew psychology, so that the fact that man gave the other creatures their names, that is their identity, was to be viewed as proof of his unquestioned ascendancy over them.

So, by this J account, man is clearly dominant, being central to the whole creation. Speaking of chapter two, Gerhard von Rad, the German biblical scholar, says, "It is man's world, the world of his life (the sown, the garden, the animals, the woman), which God in what follows establishes *around man;* and this forms the primary theme of the entire narrative, *'ādām 'a dāmā* (man—earth). . . . In this

84

world, which is regarded quite anthropocentrically, man is the first creature.''[3]

It is this view, with support from Genesis 1:27-28, the image of God and dominion verses, that Cox relies on.[4] In his reliance he joins the ranks of the orthodox who have seen this passage in a similar way for nearly two millennia.

It must be pointed out, however, that this account is only one half of the creation "witness." The other narrative, the priestly account, has a somewhat different stress. In this account the order of creation is in a different sequence, namely: vegetation, animals, man. Quite significantly, *each* of these is seen as good, and the fish and birds are specifically directed to multiply just as man is, with the implication being that multiplication applies to all forms of life. Man, to be sure, is given dominion (Genesis 1:28), but there seems to be no necessary command in this "commission" to diminish or destroy what has been previously created and pronounced good. Moreover, this P narrative has God, not man, as the center of focus. This theocentric view speaks not only of earth but also of the heavens, indeed all that is, as traceable to the creating hand of God.

From this account it is quite conceivable that the inclusionists could argue that an unchallenged

[3] Gerhard von Rad, *Genesis: A Commentary,* trans. John H. Marks (Philadelphia: Westminster Press, 1961), pp. 74-75.

[4] Cf. Cox, *The Secular City,* pp. 73-74.

man-centered view is doubtful. Certainly there is
no argument but that this account deserves as much
attention as does the other one. The P narrative is
not as old as its counterpart, to be sure, but this
very fact might illustrate its greater sophistication
and deeper insight. Without denying that man has
suzerainty and a right to use the earth, those with
an inclusive approach could claim that the earth
has meaning apart from man (God called it good
even before man was present), and further, that
use must be very carefully differentiated from abuse.
The differentiation they would determine on the
basis of ecological findings (many of which will be
discussed in the next chapter).

Such an interpretation would not be unprecedented nor one drawn from those outside Christian
circles. C. F. D Moule, the English theologian, for
instance, takes exactly such a stance in his book,
Man and Nature in the New Testament, which has
the interesting subtitle, *Some Reflections on Biblical
Ecology.* In this book Moule interprets the image
of God and dominion in terms of responsibility [5] and
stewardship, and summarizes his view by saying,

[5] It is true that Cox says that man is responsible for nature,
as he is for everything else. However, by the fact that in his
exposition of responsibility he dwells on political, economic, and
sociological problems, and that he can foresee a world city without
undue dismay, would indicate to the inclusionists that he has
no clear concept of what responsibility for nature involves, i.e.,
that he is ecologically uninformed.

Man is placed in the world by God to be its Lord. He is meant to have dominion over it and to use it . . . but only for God's sake, only like Adam in paradise, cultivating it for the Lord. As soon as he begins to use it selfishly, and reaches out to take the fruit which is forbidden by the Lord, instantly the ecological balance is upset and nature begins to groan.[6]

Now it is true that the priestly account can be interpreted differently, making it a justification for man-centeredness just as the other account is. In fact this is just what Richardson does, saying that the chronology used in this account is a literary device designed to show that what comes later in the order is to be of a higher significance. "Man as the last creature formed by God," he claims, "is also the highest creature; to him is given the right of dominion over every other created thing. All other creatures are less than man from the point of view of what is technically called 'dignity': they are all created for his sake and ordered to his good." Richardson does say that land and vegetation and animal life are good in themselves, but he goes on to qualify this by saying that they find their "proper ordering" in serving the good of man.[7] Here the connotation given the dominance of man is one more of domination than, as with Moule, responsibility.

[6] C. F. D. Moule, *Man and Nature in the New Testament* (Philadelphia: Fortress Press, 1967), p. 14.

[7] Richardson, *Toward an American Theology,* pp. 115-16.

Moule says dominion is for God's sake; Richardson says it is for man's.

With the chronological interpretation of the P account, of course, there is a reversal of the argument forwarded in connection with the J narrative. With the latter it has been held that because man is prior and names the other creatures, he is superior, while with P it is said because man is last in a kind of teleological ascension, he has the dominant position. One might ask whether in logical fairness conflicting arguments to support the same anthropocentric position can be used.

Logically fair or not, however, both arguments are forwarded, although it is noted that at least with the priestly account such arguments do not go unchallenged. The fact that there is real disagreement about these stories suggests that more than they need to be examined in order to gain a fuller biblical perspective on the whole question.

Expanding the investigation to the rest of the biblical record yields much, of course, to support those who hold that man is the central figure of attention and the rightful master of nature, with nature having no meaning apart from man. It can be pointed out that God made a specific covenant with man, and that his activity is highlighted in the historical life of a specific people, culminating in his Incarnation among those people. The prophets who served him before his coming emphasized social righteousness, the proper behavior between man and man. The Incarnation itself was God as man,[8] and not some other creature or in some other form of expression. In addition, it could be pointed out that nature not subject to man's control—the wilderness —was where the erring children of Israel had to wander and suffer and where Christ was tempted. Finally, it could be noted that a commanding figure of the kingdom come is the New Jerusalem, the city, which is the unique expression of man as opposed to nature.

With this kind of evidence the burden of proof definitely seems to be on those who would argue for a broader view. Can counter-evidence be marshalled? The answer is yes, as discovered in the work of the church historian, George H. Williams. In the preface to one of his books Williams presents a kind of compendium of the biblical evidence calling for the broader view, the biocentric perspective. Relative to the creation narratives he mentions that "man was placed in the midst of Paradise as a steward to give names to and bewonder the teeming multitudes of forms that had before him issued from the hands of the Creator." He then goes on to point out that

---

[8] Inclusionists could conceivably reply that this supports stress on the individual, since Christ was not just man but a man; God was "biologized" as an individual, not a group or a single psychosocial unit.

Noah was instructed by God to preserve from universal destruction two or seven of every kind of beast and bird, both clean and unclean, that is, without due regard to their eventual utility to man. After the Flood and the legitimation of the eating of meat, the prophets could still look forward to the restitution of peace within the animal kingdom and of harmony between man and beast. One of them, Hosea (2:18), even foresaw God entering into a covenant with the beasts of the field, the birds of the air, and the reptiles on the ground in order to secure the peace of the elect. Job (40:15) in his understandably self-centered wretchedness was reminded by God of the comfort to be gained from perspective: 'Behold now the hippopotamus which I made with thee.' Jesus said that the heavenly Father regards the lily of the field and the sparrow that falls. Paul (Romans 8:22) thought of the whole creation as in some obscure way groaning together with man in pain until the redemption. The newly discovered *Gospel According to Thomas* preserves a gospel of all creatures (1:4, 77-79) alongside the familiar gospel to all creatures (Mark 16:15).[9]

To this could be added the testimony of the psalmist concerning the care of the creatures by God (Psalm 104) as well as the fact that wilderness does not always elicit a negative response in Scripture. It was in the wilderness that the Decalogue was said to have been delivered (wilderness of the Sinai Peninsula), it was there that Elijah met God, and

[9] George H. Williams, *Wilderness and Paradise in Christian Thought* (New York: Harper, 1962), Preface, p. x.

it was the wilderness that served as the base of operations for John the Baptist.

So, obviously, evidence in support of the biocentric viewpoint is available to one who makes a point of seeking it out. Indeed, its testimony is strong enough to support a very legitimate theological position that could effectively challenge the evidence, either explicit or implicit, that sustains the exclusionists. Yet such a position is scarcely evident, and as a result the inclusionist position lacks a specifically religious focus, even though an expression of the need for such a focus has come from those with a biocentric view.

Such a need was voiced most forcibly by Aldo Leopold,[10] the conservationist, who first expressed the concept of an "ecological conscience," the heart of what he called a land ethic. Speaking of "the ethical sequence" Leopold proposed that

the first ethics dealt with the relation between individuals; the Mosaic Decalogue is an example. Later accretions dealt with the relation between the individual and society. The Golden Rule tries to integrate the in-

---

[10] Some idea of the stature of Aldo Leopold among conservationists may be gained by noting an excerpt from the *Wisconsin State Journal*, September 19, 1965, on the occasion of his being named to the National Wildlife Federation's Conservation Hall of Fame: "Aldo Leopold died in 1948, but he stands tall today, like a giant pine tree, visible from the remote corners of the land and from the concrete racetracks of civilization. His shadow has come to be the conscience of the monster ambition to make a great pinball machine of the world." (From the jacket of *Sand County Almanac*.)

dividual to society; democracy to integrate social organization to the individual.

There is yet no ethic dealing with man's relation to land and to animals and plants which grow upon it. Land, like Odysseus' slave-girls, is still property. . . .

The extension of ethics to this third element in human environment is, if I read the evidence correctly, an evolutionary possibility and an ecological necessity. It is the third step in a sequence. The first two have already been taken. Individual thinkers since the days of Ezekiel and Isaiah have asserted that the despoliation of land is not only inexpedient but wrong. Society, however, has not yet affirmed their belief.[11]

Further on, picking up this thread of development, Leopold comes to the crux of the matter:

Obligations have no meaning without conscience, and the problem we face is the extension of the social conscience from people to land.

No important change in ethics was ever accomplished without an internal change in our intellectual emphasis, loyalties, affections, and convictions. The proof that conservation has not yet touched these foundations of conduct lies in the fact that philosophy and religion have not yet heard of it.[12]

This is certainly an overstatement today (though it may not have been twenty-five years ago). Some

[11] Aldo Leopold, *A Sand County Almanac: With Other Essays on Conservation from Round River* (New York: Oxford University Press, 1966), p. 218.
[12] *Ibid.*, p. 225.

religionists have heard of conservation, and in the ecological sense Leopold proposed it. Moule writes his book on "biblical ecology," and Conrad Bonifazi has written in a vein that in large measure would have pleased Leopold. At one place Bonifazi writes:

In the light of man's thinking about the earth and his behavior upon it, the Hebrew-Christian Scriptures may also conceivably be read with new eyes, enabling us to behold there those 'sons of God' for whom creation waits: men not simply careful of their relations with each other, but who could cultivate a responsible bearing towards their natural environment; men of ecological conscience as well as social conscience, knowing themselves . . . bound up with the earth.[13]

Nevertheless, those who speak in this way are still more or less isolated individuals. There is no "school" of environmental theology. Theology still stands in the shadow of German-speaking Kantian theologians who have in the background of their thinking Newton's undeviating and impersonal mechanical universe—in spite of the fact that we live in an age of quantum physics and the principle of indeterminacy. With this view man and nature continue to be sharply differentiated,[14] thus supporting

[13] Conrad Bonifazi, *A Theology of Things* (Philadelphia: Lippincott, 1967), p. 24.
[14] Barth, for instance, wrote: "We are asserting that we have no certain information concerning the unity of our life with the life outside us" (*Die Kirchliche Dogmatik* III/4, 377 n). This is

the anthropocentric emphasis that can be derived from the biblical record. In light of this circumstance the major force of Leopold's statement stands. Therefore, the position of the inclusionists fails to pass the test in the theological realm, although, it is to be very carefully noted, this failure is by default.

Acknowledging this failure, we may ask the question as to whether the matter must end there. I for one do not believe so. And certainly the advocates of natural theology would not agree that it should. Charles Raven wrote:

> My whole contention is that nature and supernature belong together and that to divorce them, as is, alas, so freely done by our neo-orthodox theologians, is to come perilously near to the most notorious of all the early heresies. If nature is so corrupted as to be the antithesis of grace, then the Creator must be, as the Arians supposed, of a different substance from the Redeemer. . . . If grace is radically contrasted with the beauty and truth and goodness of the natural order, then any belief in a real Incarnation is impossible—unless the Christ be, as the

quoted by Santmire, "Creation and Nature," p. 124, who in his work claims that Barth is actually an agnostic as regards man's relation with nature. He goes on to say that "Barth points out [that] Christian theology should not disparage the cosmos. But this does not imply, he asserts, that Christian theology has the responsibility to articulate a comprehensive cosmology. On the contrary, it 'has neither the right nor the commission,' according to Barth, to develop a 'Christian world-view.' (*KD* III/2, 4). Thus, Barth is telling us, there is no such thing properly, as a doctrine of nature as such." "Creation and Nature," pp. 136-37.

Gnostics maintained, and their modern followers admit, a divine intruder totally other than mankind. If God is God, and God is manifested in Christ, then Creation, Redemption and Santification must be identical in origin and fundamentally also in character. It was the chief purpose of the Nicene Creed in its original form to maintain that this is the case.[15]

By this account God is to encompass the whole of reality and is not to be limited to some special area of revelatory or sanctifying activity. In such a claim Raven can point to very impressive support. Eric Rust mentions that the Hebrew mind viewed "wonders" (a possible translation of the Hebrew words *niphla'ah* and *pele,* which can also be rendered "miracles") as events covering a spectrum that to the modern mind would inappropriately include very ordinary events.

The extraordinary event was indeed just as natural as the ordinary, since all were alike the direct manifestations of the divine creative power. Hence it is not surprising to find the Old Testament classifying very ordinary phenomena as miracles. For the coming of the autumn rains, and man's supply of daily bread, could be just as miraculous as those more abnormal events that the Medieval Church associated with its saints. The Psalmist finds a "wonder" in the structure of his own body [Psalm 139: 14-16], and Job can declare that among the marvellous

[15] Charles E. Raven, *Natural Religion and Christian Theology,* (Cambridge: The University Press, 1953), pp. 2-3.

things without number which God does is the sending of
rain upon the earth [Job 5:10].[16]

This whole viewpoint carried over into what we
see recorded in the New Testament. Jesus pointed
to the activity of God in relation to sparrows, lilies
of the field, rain that fell on good and bad alike,
and seeds sown in a field—ordinary events in everyone's view. Yet by the same activity he also is at-
tested to have healed and otherwise acted in an
extraordinary way, a "miraculous" way as a modern
person would consider it. Yet, as Raven mentions,
if Christ is a focus of faith, as a unique manifesta-
tion of God, then "ordinary" and "extraordinary"
cannot be sharply separated. One can say that to
Christ either all things were wondrous (and this
is the better description) or all things were ordinary,
but stringent separation of events and processes
was not in his apperception.

This "non-separation" mentality was also present
in the Reformers. They saw God manifest in all the
operations of nature and thus viewed the "miraculous" very differently than many modern men, including modern theologians. So Calvin, as an example, could say of the "sign" of the rainbow:

If any philosophaster, to deride the simplicity of our
faith, shall contend that the variety of colours [of the

[16] Eric C. Rust, *Nature and Man in Biblical Thought* (London:
Lutterworth Press, 1953), pp. 81-82.

rainbow] arises naturally from the rays reflected by the opposite cloud, let us admit the fact, but, at the same time, deride his stupidity in not recognising God as the Lord and governor of nature, who, at his pleasure, makes all the elements subservient to his glory. If he had impressed memorials of this description on the sun, the stars, the earth, and stones, they would all have been to us as sacraments.[17]

Elsewhere Calvin points to the important analogical value of nature for the Christian faith, suggesting that attention to the activity of God in the former would help to affirm tenets of the latter. He said: "Nor would the thing [the Resurrection] be so difficult of belief were we as attentive as we ought to be to the wonders which meet our eye in every quarter of the world." [18] And, finally, commenting on Revelation 5:13 where "every creature" is seen praising the victorious Lamb, Calvin says that "it is absolutely certain, that both irrational and inanimate creatures are [here] comprehended. All, then, which is affirmed is, that every part of the universe, from the highest pinnacle of heaven to the very center of the earth, each in its own way, proclaims the glory of the Creator." [19]

At this juncture we should recall the testimony

[17] John Calvin, *Institutes of the Christian Religion*, trans. by Henry Beveridge (Grand Rapids: Eerdmans, 1957), IV/XIV, 18.

[18] *Ibid.*, III/XXV, 4.

[19] *Ibid.*, III/V, 8.

of an inclusionist like Loren Eiseley. We note that it is he, and not the exclusionists, who echoes the awareness found in the cited biblical characters and a Reformer like Calvin. Certainly he is not as specifically religious as they, and yet he sees the whole of nature in a way that can only be called religious. All life in his way of thinking, as with the Hebrew, Christ, and Calvin, is wondrous.

Now with such an array of witnesses testifying to a position that justifies a more inclusive outlook, it appears incongruous, even in this modern day of man-nature alienation, that the inclusionists' theological failure cannot be overcome. Surely the failure does not come from a lack of material and theological possibility, but rather from sheer neglect.

My own means of overcoming the failure is provided, ironically enough, by one of those whom I have designated as an exclusionist. Herbert Richardson writes, "Theology must develop a conception of God which can undergird the primary realities of the cybernetics world, viz., systems." Then he goes on to say: "And ethics must reorient its work in terms of those systems and focus on the problem of control. . . . The God of a sociotechnic intellectus [again, a context of meaning] must be reconceived as the unity of the manifold systems of the world." [20] He mentions the fact that such a conception has already been developed by American

[20] Richardson, *Toward an American Theology*, p. 23.

theologians and philosophers such as Jonathan Edwards, Ralph Waldo Emerson, Josiah Royce, and H. R. Niebuhr, and all that is required is the application of what is already at hand.

We might look at one of those whom Richardson mentions. H. R. Niebuhr, when talking about the effect of unity in God, notes that as he alone is considered holy, a kind of Puritan iconoclasm arises, casting doubts on special and holy days, places, and sites. However, he goes on to add that this phenomenon has an accompanying effect. He says,

> The counterpart of this secularization . . . is the sanctification of all things. Now every day is the day that the Lord has made; every nation is a holy people called by him into existence in its place and time and to his glory; every person is sacred, made in his image and likeness; *every living thing, on earth, in the heavens, and in the waters, is his creation and points in its existence toward him; the whole earth is filled with his glory.* (Emphasis added.) [21]

In words that are in perfect accord with those taken from Calvin, Niebuhr says everything created takes on significance; everything that makes up the manifold systems of the world is related in God. And suddenly the very important question is this: What are the manifold systems of the world? The critical

[21] H. R. Niebuhr *Radical Monotheism and Western Culture* (Lincoln: University of Nebraska Press), pp. 52-53.

answer is that *all* the systems of the world are the manifold systems, and not, for instance, the "encompassing system of social relations" to which Richardson immediately narrows his perspective after having called for a new orientation. The natural systems should be included in the calculus as well as the social, economic, political, and religious systems of the world.

The inclusionists could well agree that God is the unity of the manifold systems, the unity of "an encompassing system of relations," emphasizing that relations to be truly encompassing must include those of nature to man as well as man to man. Here can be a base for an environmental theology, which itself would undergird an environmental position that, following Richardson's suggestion, would focus on control.

To illustrate how such a view (tacitly understood by the persons involved) is applied, I shall turn to what some may feel is a mundane example,[22] but one that is very instructive. In the San Francisco Bay area one of the West Coast utilities proposed to build a nuclear reactor. By every social, political, and economic test thought to be relevant it was desirable. It would provide more power, more jobs and, of course, more wealth. Yet conservationists

[22] The example was given by Mr. David Brower, executive secretary of the Sierra Club, before a gathering of the Harvard Conservation Club, March 22, 1968.

were up in arms because of the threat of thermal pollution to the bay, a beautiful place already increasingly marred by man's "progress." With the aid of computers the conservationists calculated just what amount of thermal pollution would occur because of the reactor. Moreover, they pointed out, significantly, that the reactor was scheduled to be near the San Andreas earthquake fault that runs near San Francisco. When they presented this evidence to the bureau scheduled to grant a building permit to the utility, it was decided that the facility should not be constructed.

If only socioeconomic factors had come under consideration the reactor would have been built. But when data based on the natural factors were included the entire situation was changed. And inclusionists are inclined to say many other situations would change if *all* the pertinent factors were taken into consideration. Moreover, they could say— foreign as it sounds to modern, secularized ears— that in the case of the nuclear reactor, the presence of the San Andreas fault, manifested by the will of God as is every other part of creation, was an inherent limiting factor imposed by God and one ignored by man to his peril. (Earthquakes and floods are still designated by many as "acts of God.")

Indeed, this last type of factor has been one generally ignored in our modern approach to life. Yet if God is the unity of the systems, including nature, and man violates the systems, especially the natural one, then it follows that man in his violation is in confrontation with God. Earlier it was noted that Eiseley and other inclusionists emphasized how the emergent man who tries to extricate himself from the web of life will be subject to very dire repercussions. Interpreting this theologically we can say that where man, either because of arrogance or ignorance, lives too far out of balance with the natural order, he meets God, the author of that order as well as the Immanent One within it who binds it together, as the God of wrath and judgment. To be sure, this is a surprising and possibly repugnant position to many in an age that in large part has been given over to the glorification of man. Nevertheless, it is an implication legitimately drawn from a truly comprehensive "systems" theology.

Now it might be suggested that to adopt such a theology as Richardson proposes would be to undercut one of the elements of the inclusionists' contention, namely, the emphasis on the individual. As Richardson understands such a theology it results in a reduction of the individual in the face of the demands of the "mechanics of mass society." However, the ecologically oriented person will hasten to say that an awareness of all the systems does not reduce the need of individualism; it heightens it. At least it heightens the need for the responsible individual.[23]

As mentioned previously, the inclusionists point to their own Rachel Carson as an example of responsible individualism. She did not conform to society but rather, in an independent way, first doubted, then studied, and finally recorded the effects of pesticides. Before Miss Carson's work no computer ever indicated a possible danger in pesticides because no one feeding information into one ever presupposed a possible danger. Miss Carson indicated the danger, however, and touched off investigations that continue to grow and spread their warning.

The responsible individual is also stressed in connection with another key element in the view of those who are biocentrically oriented: population control.

[23] In his treatment of individualism Richardson fails to differentiate between the responsible kind and the irresponsible kind. When he says that "sociotechnical theology must reject that anarchic individualism which opposes all social structures in principle" (*Toward an American Theology*, p. 25), he seems to associate all individualism with that type exhibited either in late nineteenth and early twentieth-century Social Darwinism or in the contemporary radical movement. For he speaks of the opponents of sociotechnic conformism as "representatives of the new left and the old right." However, there are other kinds of individualism (though, admittedly, they may be diminishing in the United States). There is, e.g., the individualism of classical conservatism, which sees the individual not only as a recipient of rights but also as a bearer of responsibilities, one who not only has opportunities but also has duties. For a study of such conservatism see Russell Kirk, *The Conservative Mind* (Chicago: Regnery, 1960).

If population is controlled (short of mass murder or mass starvation), it appears that only responsible individuals (that is, couples) will do it. The only alternative to responsible activity on the part of individual households is some form of coercion. That coercion could take many different forms, including the possibility of the dictatorship that Huxley predicted.[24] A failure of responsible individualism and man-imposed coercion would result in the ultimate coercion of mass deaths, which would show that man was in confrontation with a wrathful God.

So, in summary, a theology with God as the unity of systems is a very definite possibility for those with an inclusive outlook, provided that it is understood that there will be a comprehensive inclusion of all systems, and that stress will be put upon the responsible individual.

[24] See note 9, pp. 67-68.

VI Determinations: Ecological and Demographic

From the home territory of the exclusionists we can proceed to that of the inclusionists. This is the area of ecological and demographic data, empirical indexes that tend to substantiate the claim that the web of life is being violated in an increasingly dangerous way. Though virtually every area of environmental studies is far from complete, there is more than enough data accumulating to illustrate why there is so much concern among life scientists. I am not a life scientist or an ecological or demographic expert; however, I do draw upon investigations and opinions of experts, the accumulative effect of which can be considered a gigantic warning signal against continuation of present trends.

While I concentrate on empirical data, I necessarily have to exclude aesthetic concerns. I do this not because aesthetics is unimportant (quite the contrary), but because aesthetics is a subject to which few are willing to grant great importance. We live in a practical, pragmatic social milieu that has lessened appreciation of the intangible. In our day one person may stand at the rim of the Grand Canyon and gaze in true wonder, while another (whom I once observed) may look upon it for the first time and blurt out, "Man, what an ashtray!"

The same sort of thing may occur with marshland or meadowland. Some may see in such an area something intrinsically beautiful and valuable, or like Eiseley, possibly be brought to an awareness of the Unseen. Others, especially in America, will react in a way described by Ashley Montagu, who himself clearly is not in sympathy with them. "There are men in America," says Montagu, "who on perceiving a green field or a meadow begin to slaver at the gills and, like Uriah Heep, start washing their hands with invisible soap at the contemplation of the thought, nay, the beatific vision, of a glorious development on the site of a four-lane concrete highway, with all the trees cut down, the ponds and streams filled in, and lovely gas stations, hotdog stands and billboards usefully replacing all the land that was going to waste." [1]

Aesthetics is very often crowded out by utilitarian concerns, economic interests, and what is popularly called progress. Those for whom such practical areas are all-important can be swayed only by empirical data that prove indisputable, either to aesthetes or non-aesthetes. So, while a brown cloud of smog hanging over a city may leave some people indifferent (even though it causes revulsion on the part of sensitive persons), these indifferent people will become very interested if it is shown that smog is a direct cause of cancerous conditions in human beings. If it is a question only of smog being pretty or not, it will not be important to many; if the question is whether it is deadly or not, then everyone is interested.

The considerations discussed below are not as clear-cut as a direct connection between smog and cancer would be. They are, comparatively speaking, first findings, because of the fact that environmental studies, up to the very recent past, have always been in a secondary, scrambling position. However, the considerations are both numerous enough and ominous enough to confirm the fact that man has approached an ecologic crisis which, if he does not correctly deal with it, will, as it were, deal with him.

[1] Ashley Montagu, *The American Way of Life* (New York: Putnam's, 1967), p. 103.

(1) The fundamental place to begin is in connection with population. Viewing the earth as the biosphere, we note that one species is dominant, both in activity and numbers; that species is *Homo sapiens*. It is increasing roughly at 2.0 percent per year,[2] meaning that it will double its number in 35 years. Such an increase will put its 3.479 billion[3] at something near 7 billion shortly after the turn of the century. At present it is estimated that one billion persons are undernourished, and an additional 800 million are deficient in one or several key nutrients,[4] so that more than half of humanity suffers from at least malnourishment.

In ecological terms anytime a species in a defined area has insufficient food for half or more of its numbers it is considered in imbalance. This is just the circumstance of humanity on earth. Moreover, as the Special Task Force on Environmental Health reported to the Department of Health, Education and Welfare of the U.S. Government: "Virtually every assessment of environmental problems attributed them, in substantial measure, to the combined effects of increasing population (particularly urban population) and industrialization."[5] This is

[2] From World Population Data Sheet, Population Reference Bureau, Washington, D.C., March, 1968.

[3] *Ibid.*

[4] Georg Borgstrom, *The Hungry Planet* (New York: Macmillan, Collier Books, 1967), Intro., XI.

[5] *A Strategy for a Livable Environment,* p. 16.

why those with an inclusionist approach are upset with Cox's prediction of a world city, and cringe from what they consider the spector of "the almost solid mass of hominised substance" that Teilhard visualizes.

(2) Increasing population leads to increased urbanization, and urbanization is actually a two-step phenomenon. First, people are born into or come into the city and, second, they spread the perimeter of the city in every-widening circles or increase its bounds along ever-lengthening projections. Thus there is the phenomenon of urban sprawl, some of it quality, some of it resulting in "slurbs" (half suburb, half slum). In either case the result is the taking over of land. One of the inclusionists comments on this aspect by saying,

The problem is an enormous one both in extent and speed of change. Three hundred million Americans are expected to populate the United States in the year 2000. If indeed 80% of these will live in urban places, then this involves the urbanisation of 55,000,000 acres of non-urbanised land. If one extrapolates from the present Megalopolis to this future population, then 10% of the land area of the United States, 200 million acres, will fall within urban influence, comparable to Megalopolis, in a mere 35 years.[6]

[6] Ian McHarg, "Ecological Determinism" (paper prepared for Department of Landscape Architecture, University of Pennsylvania, n.d.), p. 2.

How this sprawl may influence just one state was offered by a popular writer as he wrote about California. He noted that that state produces 25 percent of the nation's table food, 43 percent of its fresh vegetables, and 42 percent of its nut and fruit crops. And by conservative estimate, half of California's prime cropland will go to housing and industry in the next third of a century. The writer adds that the pessimists feel that up to 80 percent of the prime land will go in that time period.[7]

Switching to the other end of the country, we can see another aspect of urban sprawl. From Greater Boston there was an example of how disruption of natural systems results in a rebound upon those who accomplish the disruption. The rebound upon Greater Boston took the form of floods. In March, 1968, the area experienced very heavy rainfall, and several towns of the metropolitan area were inundated with rising waters. It happens that many of these towns were partially built on swamp and marsh areas that the Department of Natural Resources of the Commonwealth had suggested be avoided. Their suggestion had been made no less than seven years prior to the flood.[8]

And, of course, the spread of the cities means a proportionate reduction in the habitat of nonhuman

[7] David Lyle, ''The Human Race Has, Maybe, Thirty-five Years Left,'' *Esquire*, September, 1967.

[8] *Boston Globe*, March 24, 1968, pp. 1-23.

life forms, thus further decreasing the diversity of taxa that ecologists feel are beneficial.

(3) One widely recognized and environmental problem closely allied to cities is that of air pollution. A persistent claim is that the biggest cause of this problem is that most outstanding example of man-and-machine, the automobile. In a report that has been mentioned before, it is noted that

this year [1967], the 90,000,000 automobiles in use will burn an estimated 60,000,000,000 gallons of gasoline, or about 700 gallons for the typical automobile. This means that each automobile in the country will discharge in a single year over 1,600 pounds of carbon monoxide, 230 pounds of hydrocarbons, and 77 pounds of oxides of nitrogen.[9]

All these discharged substances, of course, are pollutants. Something is being done about this, to be sure. As a slightly earlier report said: "The hydrocarbon emission from the crankcase, about 30% of the total, will in the foreseeable future be nearly 100% controlled." Yet it went on to say: "However, considering the difficulty of enforcement and effective inspection, we may not reach more than a 50% reduction of the other emissions." A further damper is put on when the reports say:

It is predicted that the increase in automobile population will continue with the same rate for many years. . . .

[9] *A Strategy for a Livable Environment*, p. 5.

By 1980 the use of gasoline in the Los Angeles area [e.g.] will have increased by a factor of four since smog was first noticed around 1945. Parallel with the increase of fuel is the emission of pollutants. The partial control of emission predicted for the coming years cannot keep up with the increase.[10]

This same report mentions a somewhat lesser known aspect of the air pollution problem—the effect of carbon dioxide on the atmosphere. It mentions that the burning of coal, oil, and natural gas is going on at the rate of 6 billions tons a year. At this rate there will be 25 percent more CO_2 in the atmosphere in the year 2000 than there is now. This could well modify the best balance of the atmosphere to the degree that climate changes would occur that would be beyond even national control.[11] The overall result of increased CO_2 in the air is a general heating of the atmosphere. Calculating what could happen to the antarctic ice cap as a result of this heating, it is conceivable that the runoff could raise the sea level some 4 feet every 10 years, 40 feet per century.[12] This would, of course, cause devastation to the coastal areas of the world.

[10] *Restoring the Quality of Our Environment: Report of the Environmental Pollution Panel, President's Science Advisory Committee* (Washington D.C.: Government Printing Office, 1965), pp. 67-68.

[11] *Ibid.*, p. 9.

[12] *Ibid.*, p. 123.

In still another aspect of air pollution there may arise a situation whereby the problem is not an unwelcome addition to the atmosphere but a depletion of its vital property. As an editorial in *The Christian Century* put it:

> According to scientist Lamont C. Cole of Cornell University, the human community is in danger of running out of oxygen. Oxygen shortage has occasionally been shown to exist in the United States, Japan and Great Britain. Although the worldwide circulation of air, which is about 20 per cent oxygen, makes up for local shortages, it may not continue to do so unless some thought is given to conserving oxygen-producing vegetation. The chance sinking of a few tankers carrying plant poisons could seriously diminish the capacity of sea plants—the source of 70 per cent of the earth's oxygen—to supply this vital element. The destruction of rain forests by heedless industrialization could have the same effect. Professor Cole points out that the increase of human and animal population, the spread of fires and the destruction of greenery push us all toward the danger point.[13]

The mention of the chance sinking of ships is not irrelevant. The breakup of oil-bearing ships in the oceans, causing widespread oil pollution, became. a far too frequent occurrence in the 1960's. Such chance happenings point to a very important part of ecological considerations, the weak-link aspect, soon to be discussed.

[13] *The Christian Century,* January 17, 1968, p. 69.

Finally, it is to be noticed that though no conclusive direct relationship has been established between polluted air and cancer, as was mentioned in a previous hypothetical example, there have been interesting inferences drawn from the increase of lung cancer in areas of greater population concentration, that is, where air pollution is greater. In the United States the number of lung cancer deaths per 100,000 population averages 15 in rural areas, 18 in cities of less than 250,000, 22 in cities having from 250,000 to 1,000,000 persons, and 30 in cities having a population greater than 1,000,000.[14] This, again, is far from conclusive, but no one can deny it is suggestive.

(4) Pollution of the air is being matched if not exceeded by the pollution of water, at least in the industrialized countries. And, as in other areas, the industrial leader, the United States, serves as the outstanding example.

Dr. Commoner, citing a report to the Federal Council for Science and Technology by the Committee on Pollution in 1966, says "among other things the report points out that at the present rate of accumulation of pollutants, essentially all of the surface waters of the United States will become so contaminated as to lose their biological capability for purification within the next twenty years."[15]

---

[14] *A Strategy for a Livable Environment*, p. 11.
[15] Commoner, *Science and Survival*, p. 144 (note 3).

Of course, water is treated to make it fit for human consumption and other uses, and with increasing pollution the demands for treatment increase. In connection with that it might be noted what the present condition of water treatment is. The Task Force on Environmental Health claimed that fifty million Americans drink water that does not meet Public Health Service drinking water standards.[16] Without strenuous efforts in the face of increased demands the situation, obviously, can only get worse.

(5) Another kind of pollution is that which has arisen in the last 25 years, the contamination arising from radioactivity. This occurs not only from the nuclear blasts that have been detonated but also, and more importantly, from the present and potential nuclear reactors, or, more specifically, the wastes they produce which must be disposed of. One learned estimate is that by 1980 reactor waste production will be in the neighborhood of 500 billion curies, up from a virtual zero in 1945.[17] And all this production is going on when the only feasible means of disposal are burying, which, obviously, can only go on so long, and dumping in the sea, a very questionable practice, especially since many view the sea as the last great hope to feed mankind's bloated population.

Ironically enough, it should be mentioned that

[16] *A Strategy for a Livable Environment*, p. 13.
[17] *Ibid.*, p. 23.

some of the call for nuclear reactors comes from those who want nuclear power to replace coal or oil-fired electric generating units, which presently add so much to air pollution.

Other sources of radiation include X-ray units, of which there are 210,000 in the United States,[18] and radon gas produced in the mines where uranium ore is extracted. The full effect of these is not known, though of the latter it is claimed that exposures to it have caused an increased incidence of lung cancer in the mines.[19]

(6) Of course, radioactive waste is only one of many kinds that must be disposed of. There is also the so-called third pollutant (after air and water pollutants), the solid waste accumulation, or trash. In America over 200 million tons of trash are generated per year at present.[20] Forty million old automobiles are rusting in junkyards or miscellaneous places. As of 1965, 4.5 pounds of solid waste were generated per person per day. If present trends continue the amount generated will be 18.0 pounds per person per day by A.D. 2000. And this, it is to be remembered, coming from a population nearly twice the size of what it was in 1965.

Not all solid waste, naturally, is kept in solid

[18] *Ibid.*, p. 22.
[19] *Ibid.*, p. 23.
[20] All the facts given in this section come from a lecture given by Dr. Joseph Harrington, Assistant Professor of Health Engineering, Harvard University, September 29, 1967.

form. Some of it is buried, some is incinerated. Here, however, one appreciates interactions of different ecological problems. Burying of waste takes large amounts of land out of use, while incineration adds to the problem of air pollution.

(7) While the third pollutant is very visible, what could be called a fourth pollutant cannot be seen at all. However, it can be heard; indeed, that is the problem. Noise pollution has not been subject to many exact measurements, primarily because its threat has only recently been recognized. Moreover, the definition of what is too much sound will vary between a quiet, reserved person and a teen-ager who listens to the scream of modern music.

One noise threat that can be definitely specified, however, is the one that is connected with the proposed supersonic transport, known as SST. Dr. Paul Ehrlich mentions that if as many as 175 of these planes were to fly along domestic air routes, the people within hearing distance, that is, along the routes, would be subject to someting like 700 sonic booms a day.[21] Such a condition as that is quite beyond human tolerance. Indeed it is questionable as to whether humans can endure more than a few sonic booms within a specified time, at least on a regular basis.

(8) When I spoke of solid waste accumulation

[21] Paul Ehrlich, *The Population Bomb* (New York: Ballantine Books, 1968), p. 129.

ecological interactions were mentioned, and such interactions bring us to the most telling argument of those who approach matters ecologically. They emphasize interactions and highlight those which are unforeseen. I would characterize this as the "weak-link" aspect of environmental situations. There are many examples.

It has already been mentioned how widespread death control was not accompanied by birth control in connection with the worldwide public health measures taken after World War II. Birth control was the weak link. Another example comes from nuclear weapons testing. Much of this was done before the actual extent of fallout was known. To cite a specific instance:

In 1956 AEC [Atomic Energy Commission] Commissioner W. F. Libby predicted that nuclear tests carried out through May, 1954, would deposit in United States soil a maximum of 7 millicuries of strontium-90 per square mile. But actual measurements by the AEC showed that the average strontium-90 content of U.S. soil had reached about 47 millicuries per square mile in 1958, although the total amount of testing had only about doubled since 1954.[22]

Thus, either the original prediction was greatly in error, or the fallout increased at an exponential

[22] Commoner, *Science and Survival*, p. 17.

rate. In either case the results were wholly unexpected.

Another example comes from the use of pesticides. When pesticides first came into use they were hailed as a panacea and widely used. In fact, they may be the reason why a country such as the United States can feed its 200 million-plus people better than any other nation—that is, on the average. Still for all their use and admitted benefit considerable doubts have been raised about them. R. L. Rudd, who took up the work begun by Rachel Carson, would agree that pesticides have done some good but points to several different items that might be considered weak links in their use. Some of these are:

1. Most pesticides are nonselective, i.e., they kill more than the intended victim or victims;

2. Their manner of use is imprecise, i.e., they are broadcast over wide areas rather than carefully directed toward specific targets.

3. Many kinds of chemicals used (especially chlorinated hydrocarbons such as DDT) are stable and survive in soil, water, and living tissue;

4. Many of the chemicals follow insidious routes such as those of delayed toxicity, secondary poisoning, etc. Thus the insecticides which kill, say, pests in a body of water may also kill fish which eat the pests as well as men who eat the fish.[23]

[23] R. L. Rudd, *Pesticides in the Living Landscape* (Madison: University of Wisconsin Press, 1964), pp. 3-6, 43-56, 248-67.

The extent of the weak link of DDT stability in living tissue is illustrated by Dr. Ehrlich when he mentions that among Americans the pesticide averages eleven parts per million in fatty tissues. This is not the highest of readings found, however; Israelis have been found to have over nineteen parts per million.[24]

Pesticides are an example of substances that were used before their full effect was even guessed. But pesticides hardly stand alone. "The Food and Drug Administration has estimated that the American people are being exposed to some 500,000 different substances, many of them over long periods of time. Yet fewer than ten per cent of these substances have been catalogued in a manner that might provide the basis for determining their effects on man and his environment."[25]

Another kind of tack is taken by an ecologist who touches upon the artificial society mentioned by one of the exclusionists. He remarks how

There is good reason to believe that people could be conditioned to adjust themselves to a highly artificial technologically controlled environment such as the city under a plastic bubble which some envision. Such an arrangement, however, could not only congeal the pattern of living, but be vulnerable on two counts. The greater our dependence upon an elaborate chain of technology

[24] Ehrlich, *The Population Bomb*, p. 52.
[25] *A Strategy for a Livable Environment*, p. 5.

the more liable we become to disaster through failure of any link. And the more restricted our range of experience, even though physical needs are met, the greater our loss of flexibility to meet emergency. The too-sheltered child is an example. So is battery-grown poultry. These birds, raised under completely controlled conditions, must be protected against sudden noises or even the presence of a stranger. Otherwise they pile up in a corner and smother each other.[26]

Such an account might be dismissed as reactionary if there were no examples to suggest that it might be true. But in fact there are such examples. In November, 1965, all the electric power in an 80,000-square-mile area of the northeastern United States and Canada failed. The incident that triggered the

[26] Paul B. Sears, "Utopia and the Living Landscape," *Daedalus*, Spring, 1965, p. 484. Though it is admitted by the inclusionists that a highly artificial environment is feasible, they tend to deny that a wholly artificial one such as Richardson foresees is possible. Thus, e.g., McHarg says, "While there can be no completely natural environments inhabited by man, completely artificial environments are equally unlikely. Man in common with all organisms is a persistent configuration of matter through which the environment ebbs and flows continuously. Mechanically, he exchanges his substance at a very rapid rate while, additionally, his conceptions of reality are dependent upon the attribution of meaning to myriads of environmental stimuli which impinge upon him continuously. The materials of his being are natural, as are many of the stimuli which he perceives; his utilization of the materials and of many stimuli is involuntary. Man makes artifices, but galactic and solar energy, gases of hydrosphere and atmosphere, the substance of the lithosphere, and all organic systems remain elusive of human artificers." "The Place of Nature in the City of Man," p. 11.

entire blackout was the failure of one relay that fed into a feeder line in one small part of the vast electrical network covering the affected area. The blackout was something that simply was not supposed to happen. It did. Speaking of the incident, Commoner notes that, "Although the 'cause' of the blackout has been discovered in the sense that the failure began with the opening of an incorrectly set relay at Queenston, Ontario, the crucial point is that no one yet knows why that failure precipitated the spreading disaster. In other words, the power network was established before anyone understood the circumstances under which it would fail." [27]

Another kind of artificial power network one can think of is the blanket of aircraft and submarines carrying nuclear weapons throughout the world. Here, too, is a system that is not supposed to fail. Yet in the last few years planes carrying these weapons have been lost on two different occasions. No explosions ensued, to be sure, and it is claimed that they cannot occur. The Northeastern power network also was not supposed to fail. [28]

[27] Commoner, *Science and Survival*, p. 135, note 1.

[28] The weak-link aspect is the part of ecological considerations which most militates against the kind of pragmatic approach generally supported by Cox. Of course, it is not possible for men to know everything that will occur as a result of their actions, but it does seem clear that in the future, at least in connection with environmental matters, man will have to proceed with more caution and a more comprehensive outlook. Too often in the past, "solutions" of problems have turned out to be no more than the initiators of worse problems. Again the popula-

(9) Returning to more natural systems, we shall consider two areas that, unlike many others, have received much attention and are subject to many conservation measures. I refer to forests and soil.

With all the attention forests have received the fact remains that conditions are something like this:

At one time forests covered nearly 15 billion acres of land. But men have consumed and destroyed trees far more rapidly than the trees have been replaced by nature, with the result that approximately one-third of the original forests have disappeared. In most industrial countries wood is still being consumed more rapidly than it is being replaced by new growth—in Europe and America at a rate between 10 and 15 per cent faster than the rate of replacement.[29]

It has been over a decade since Harrison Brown wrote this summary statement, but in this age of the increasing three P's—that is, population, processes, and products—it is extremely unlikely that the situation has changed, at least for the better.

tion problem is a prime example. The "solution" of the disease problem led to unprecedented growth in human numbers. As a result of that, man is now desperately seeking means to dramatically raise food production. If, somehow, that problem is "solved," the question remains as to what effect the raising of new crops will have on the interrelated biological systems. In light of such things as the harmful effects of pesticides, the way fertilizers pollute natural water systems, and the vulnerability of monocultural landscapes, it could be that the "solution" of the food problem will end up as a disastrous "final solution."

[29] Brown, *The Challenge of Man's Future*, p. 128.

Ecologists repeatedly point to the fact that historical geography has revealed that deforestation has had profound effects on civilization.[30] It is known, for instance, that the lands of the Mediterranean Basin were not always as barren as they are now. They had forests at one time, and it was only with the demise of the trees that aridity set in. This, of course, is but one example of the importance of trees in the entire processes of photosynthesis and weather control.

As for soil, the summary statement, at least for the U.S., again comes from the pen of Brown. He wrote,

Dr. Hugh H. Bennett, former chief of the Soil Conservation Service of the U.S. Department of Agriculture, has estimated that during the short life of the United States approximately 280 million acres of crop and range land have been essentially destroyed, and that about 100 million acres have been so badly damaged by erosion that they cannot be restored. Altogether it is estimated that of the original average 9 inches of top soil in existence when the nation was founded, approximately one-third has been washed away. If the process is left to nature, every inch thus lost can be replaced only by many centuries of geologic and biologic activity.[31]

[30] Cf. Clarence Glacken, ''Changing Ideas of the Habitable World,'' *Man's Role in Changing the Face of the Earth*, ed. Wm. L. Thomas, Jr. (Chicago: University of Chicago Press, 1956), pp. 70-88.

[31] Brown, *The Challenge of Man's Future*, pp. 132-33.

It might be suggested that soil loss and depletion are not as important as they once were, since we live in a day of miracle foods and artificial concoctions. However, Roger Revelle, director of Harvard's Center for Population Studies, reminds us that agricultural processes are still the best way to utilize solar energy and to convert it into edible foodstuffs.[32]

(10) Not only are trees being cut down by man, but nonhuman animal life as well. An examination of the extirpation of animal species, part of the "passing phase" of brutalization to which Cox has reference, is a sad, bloody chapter in history. As far back as 1945 it was written that

during [the] period of approximately 2000 years [i.e., the Christian Era] the world has lost through extinction about 106 known forms of mammals. About 28 per cent of these are subspecies of still existing species; but the full species completely and irretrievably lost number approximately 77.

Between A.D. 1 and 1800 about 33 mammals are more or less definitely known to have become extinct. . . . Each half-century period since 1800 shows a steadily increasing rate of extinction. The last 100 years has witnessed the passing of about 67 per cent of the 106 extinct forms.[33]

[32] This reminder was given by Dr. Revelle in a lecture at Harvard's School for Public Health, October 9, 1967.

[33] Francis Harper, *Extinct and Vanishing Mammals of the Old World* (New York: American Committee for International Wildlife Protection, 1945), p. 8.

The World Wildlife Fund has indicated that fifty species of wildlife have vanished from the American scene in the last fifty years, and that worldwide there are at least one hundred species of mammals, birds, and fish in danger of extinction.[34]

It is true that anthropocentric man might note that animal species became extinct even before man appeared on the scene. However, this argument fails to take two factors into account. Extinction of species in the past took vast stretches of time, and other species were always evolving. The extirpations going on now are taking place in a veritable twinkling of an eye, geologically speaking, and only one species is succeeding those being slaughtered—the killer himself, man. Of course, self-centered man may see the passing of other species as of no consequence, since he feels that only man has value. Yet the ecologist, having observed that health (that is, stability) in natural systems results from a diversity of interacting species, feels very ill at ease at the prospect of a diminution of species and the superdomination of just one. It may be that Christian man, remembering that his Lord said that God had regard even for a sparrow, also feels somewhat ill at ease.

(11) A final area of ecological relevance is to be found in connection with the effect, that is, the stress, created by crowded areas. Experiments on ani-

---

[34] *Boston Globe*, April 2, 1968, p. 56.

mals have shown that aberrant behavior does arise when they are subjected to overcrowding. The most famous of these experiments was carried out by researcher John B. Calhoun with his study of rats.[35] Whether these kinds of experiments are analogous to the human situation is still being debated. However, it can be wondered whether the analogy should be doubted. All one has to do is to observe or read of the activity in the crowded American cities of today, and he will note a panorama of aberrant behavior. Here is an illustration, as Huxley would put it, of the big-brained mammal proving that he is not capable of forming an organism, but only capable of forming an organization;[36] and in crowded metropolitan areas the organization is poor and often perverse.

Other areas could be touched upon, but the point has been made. With the kind of evidence presented here the inclusionists have no doubt that present trends must be altered, and in a dramatic fashion. Token steps will not be enough, for the interplay of so many bad trends is leading to disaster; major changes in approach and procedure are required. A lack of such changes will mean the end of civilization as we know it. As David M. Gates, director of the Missouri Botanical Gardens put it, testifying before

[35] Cf. John C. Calhoun, ''Population Density and Social Pathology,'' *Scientific American*, February, 1962, pp. 139 f.

[36] See note 9, pp. 67-68.

a House subcommittee on science and technology: "We do not understand the dynamics of a forest, grassland, ocean, lake, pond or river, nor are we proceeding rapidly enough toward this understanding. We will go down in history as an elegant technological society struck down by biological disintegration for lack of ecological understanding." [37]

[37] *New York Times*, March 20, 1968, p. 14.

VII Conclusions

As any half-discerning reader has already guessed,
I hold that the position of the inclusionists is by
far the more valid position of those I have con-
trasted. In the preceding study I have attempted
to be thorough and accurate but certainly not ob-
jective in the sense of being neutral. One cannot
be neutral when the choices are as distinct as those
which mark the inclusionists and exclusionists. I
can specify why my allegiance lies with those having
the more inclusive view by turning to the issues
at stake as they were outlined in the Introduction.

First, turning to the question of control, it is plain

that the exclusionists, buttressed by the dominant Christian view of the separation of man and nature and the general cultural position[1] that has been informed by that view, have neglected to take all relevant factors into consideration. This is not surprising, since up to this very time social, political, economic, religious, and virtually all other interests could be dealt with most of the time apart from the biological context in which they took place. To be sure, it is felt that certain ancient civilizations may have declined because of ecological abuse, but in the modern era it has been possible to presuppose that the needed "biological support" would be there.

This is no longer the case, however. As Commoner puts it, in connection with the various pollution problems: "We have come to the turning point in the human habitation of the earth. The environment is a complex, subtly balanced system, and it is this integrated whole which receives the impact of all the separate insults inflicted by pollutants. . . . I believe that the cumulative effects of these pollutants, their interactions and amplification, can be fatal to the complex fabric of the biosphere."[2]

Man has pushed up to limits inherent in the given system. He has been able to claim ever-increasing control because the limit was not yet in sight. *This ability has deceived him into believing that there is*

[1] I shall deal with that position and the needed reaction to it in the next chapter.

[2] Commoner, *Science and Survival*, p. 122.

no limit to his control or at least no countervailing force against his activity. But as the ecological indexes show, the limitations are there.

If one could speak of two or three areas of ecological concern only, there might be room for considerable debate, but when one can specify nearly a dozen areas (and, again, these should be thought of not only separately but in interaction and coincidental effect, that is, as they really operate), then debate appears gratuitous. The ecological data promise reverberation with a continuation of present trends, not to mention new unbridled projects of man. And, as I have already indicated, interpreted theologically, it can be said that man in his uninformed quest for dominance will finally meet God, not in anticipation of a great synthesis as Teilhard would have it, but as the reality of the systems over which man seeks control, and in a wrathful expression of sovereignty.

Apart from this consideration of control and what man can and cannot do, there is the question of what man should and should not do. This has to do with the second issue that was mentioned, the one revolving around the question of the proper response to the natural order. It is an even more fundamental question than the one concerning control, for even if man could impose his will upon nature in an unlimited way, or at least arrive at the "hermetically sealed" society of which Mumford speaks and Richardson more than hints, there would remain the query as to whether he should do so.

In their various ways the exclusionists have said yes to such a query, as have all those whom they represent, the majority that separate man and nature. Man in their view is the measure of all value in creation, and they stand with the prevailing opinion of two thousand years behind them. Yet I have shown that the man-centered emphasis can be effectively challenged, and with material (such as scriptural material) from the very sources that undergird the exclusionists. Anthropocentrism is a bias, and like all bias it becomes highly selective in its choice of references and emphases. Thus Teilhard begins his study with man as the focus, Richardson excludes biological considerations, and Cox emphasizes the Yahwistic account of creation. This is not to say that much of what the exclusionists present is unimportant. Man is of value, he does have a greater consciousness than other beings, he has been and is the object of divine grace. The inclusionists do not question this. Indeed, with their emphasis on the uniqueness of the individual, they attribute a kind of importance to the human being that the collectivism of Teilhard or Richardson is not inclined to do.

The difference lies in the fact that the inclusionists say that value pervades all of life, and not just its human expression. An insect, a bird, a beast, are all important *as such*. Looking at their position theologically we note that Jesus said God had regard for a sparrow. The point is that God regards the sparrow *qua* sparrow and not as some bird that man might see or somehow use. If a flower in the desert grows, blooms, and dies, is it of no significance because man did not see it? I would claim that this is in no way true. The flower is of value, for God made it and sees it.

Another aspect of response to nature has to do with the perception derivable from it. The psalmist, John Ruskin, and Loren Eiseley are three men over the centuries who have sensed the presence of the divine in nature. It is an irony of our modern day that one finds a "secular" scientist expressing a type of religious consciousness that influential theologians are inclined to dismiss. It is Eiseley for whom the biblical bush still burns, while, say, for a Cox the light has been extinguished. The question is whether the influence of those for whom the light has gone out will prevail, and thus eliminate all possibility of an awareness of the numinous in those who are capable of response. Certainly in Teilhard's "involuted" world, Richardson's wholly artificial society, or Cox's world city, the possibility of a numinous experience from nature will be practically nil.

I hold that to support activities that would close

off a channel of religious awareness is a spiritual outrage, comparable to the destruction of food-stuffs that might otherwise nurture a man physically. To recall what was said earlier, men, or at least some men, do not live by bread alone, and to destroy or completely alter a context in which otherwise they could know the mysterious hand of God is a violation that should not be allowed.

Finally, there is the question of the proper perspective on man and whether he is best considered as apart from or bound up with the environment. The answer is somewhat complex. Too often, the complexity has been missed, and this oversight led to simplistic answers such as that man stands wholly apart from nature or that man is no more than an advanced ape. Man is a biological being who, in a way not understood, has a power of abstraction and a spiritual consciousness. In his mind man can completely transcend the natural order, "rearrange" reality by means of his imagination, and project his thought through both past and future time.

In all these ways man stands over against environment. In this he has a godlike power. Yet at the same time this mind-being is biological, fixed in space, and subject to exterior powers and influences. As such he is no more than an aspect of the whole physical reality, and is subject to the workings of that reality as are all other aspects of it. It is precisely the confusion of the vast vistas of the mind with the sharply circumscribed reality of man, the biological entity, that has caused the problem in connection with the question of control. Too often there has been a facile equation between the mind's conception and the biological being's expression, without a prior question of whether such an equation should be formed.

Thus it can be seen that man is both apart from and part of the environment. This fact requires a degree of sophistication as to how man proceeds. He can express his uniqueness in a variety of ways —music, art, poetry, philosophy, literature, worship of God, even invention and manipulation within limits—but he cannot pose as unique in the area of the biological, for he is of the earth, earthly. This is all, really, that the inclusionists are trying to say.

Because man continues to act as though he were unique in the biological realm the entire earth is entering into an advanced stage of the ecological crisis. The stage has been reached because of unrelenting increases in population and pollution. Accompanying this crisis is an emerging crisis of values, which includes dominant religious values. Richardson has correctly sensed that a fundmental change in the overall structure of civilization is required. However, in contrast to his prophecy I hold that sociotechnics is not the first stage of a new era but the last stage of an old era. Cybernetics is the latest expression of man, the tinkering primate. There is nothing essentially new in cybernetics; the machines are simply more complicated.

To have a truly new era requires that there be prevailing attitudes and values that contrast markedly with those which have prevailed heretofore. These attitudes and values need not be new in the sense that they have not been previously known or even practiced to some degree. The newness comes, rather, from their emergence from their secondary position and their assumption of the dominant role. When this occurs the invisible doorway of which Eiseley speaks can swing open, and a truly new era can begin. The task at hand is to specify such attitudes and values and to tell how they should be implemented.

VIII   Proposals

The new values, or better, value-orientations[1] that must achieve dominance will, as said, contrast with those which presently prevail. This is because at present the prevailing attitudes are ones that are far more amenable to the exclusionist rather than the inclusionist approach. I have chosen a highly recognized American sociologist [2] as my source for major American value-orientations, and I would con-

[1] Where a value may be considered an abstract ideal or model, a value-orientation is a combination of the abstract and the concrete. A value-orientation is, simply put, an applied value, a position held resulting in a particular mode of behavior.

[2] Robin M. Williams, Jr., writing in his *American Society* (New York: Knopf, 2nd ed., rev., 1967). I have drawn on Chapter XI of the book, ''Values and Beliefs in American Society,'' pp. 415-70.

tend that, at least in relations with the natural order, what you find with the American you find with other Western men (though possibly to lesser degrees).

Our sociologist lists fifteen major value-orientations as follows:

1. Achievement and Success
2. Activity and Work
3. Moral Orientation
4. Humanitarian Mores
5. Efficiency and Practicability
6. Progress
7. Material Comfort
8. Equality
9. Freedom
10. External Conformity
11. Science and Secular Rationality
12. Nationalism-Patriotism
13. Democracy
14. Individual Personality
15. Racism and Relation Group—Superiority Themes

The social scientist found that the overall impact of these value-orientations could be summarized in several generalizations. Those pertinent to the man-nature relation are these:

(1) American culture is organized around the attempt at *active mastery* rather than *passive acceptance*.

(2) It tends to be interested in the *external world*

of things and events, of the palpable and immediate, rather than in the inner experience of meaning and affect. *Its genius is manipulative rather than contemplative.* (Last emphasis added.)

(3) Its world-view tends to be *open* rather than closed: it emphasizes change, flux, movement.[3]

Putting together emphasized words from these three generalizations, we can see that American culture emphasizes active mastery of the external world, which is seen as open, i.e., subject to infinite change. That is another way of saying the culture emphasizes the absolute control of nature. The above list confirms that America is morally oriented, but the orientation is humanitarian, or in terms I have been using, anthropocentric. Nature, as Aldo Leopold noted, is not in the moral calculus.

The emphasis on man and his dominance of nature has brought the Western nations to world-ascendancy, with the United States foremost among them. With such success in the background the task and challenge of changing prevailing Western attitudes is obvious. Some observers, noting the ominous ecological indexes, have suggested that Western man must look to the East with its more reflective views that stress contemplation and closeness to nature. These, somehow, are to replace the subjugation views, which are now so prevalent.

[3] *Ibid.*, p. 469.

I doubt if this position holds much promise, however. In virtually every confrontation between Western and Eastern positions, at least so far as the man-nature relation is concerned, the West has prevailed. Easterners were not so otherworldly or contemplative as to refuse medical assistance, which reduced their death rate, nor did they control themselves in such a way as to reduce their birthrate. Thus the non-Western world finds itself in even more desperate straits than the West, because it accepted short-term death control while being even worse than the West in practicing adequate birth control. Besides, we have been told often that the non-Western nations are now in a "revolution of rising expectations." Translated, that means that they want to be as materially satisfied as are many Westerners. Seemingly their more mystic views, stressing harmony with nature, have been no match for the influence of technological, acquisitive Western society.

Instead of substituting Eastern attitudes for Western ones, I contend that what is needed is the substitution of minor Western positions for what are presently the major ones. I have already shown how testimony supporting harmony between man and nature can be derived from biblical and historical sources, and how it can take doctrinal form within a systems theology. An emphasis upon this kind of theology could lead to a full-blown school of environmental theology[4] that could challenge and finally replace the theological justifications for subjugation that presently prevail. With this new theology, to take just one example, the ruling conceptions of Genesis, especially the dominance as domination and "be fruitful and multiply" views, would be seen, at best, as fulfilled injunctions.

Apart from theology, there are many other, currently minor, forces that could emerge and alter the present man-nature alienation. For instance, included in the list of value-orientations given above is an emphasis on the individual personality. This links up with a major inclusionist emphasis and could be an important bridge over which inclusionist positions could proceed from a minor to a major influence. Of course, involved with this movement would be the requirement that emphasis be put upon the responsible, knowledgeable individual, and not upon the individual per se. This emphasis would

[4] Besides the works of Moule and Bonifazi, other examples of an emerging theological interest in environmental problems are: Joseph Sittler, "A Theology for Earth," *The Christian Scholar*, June, 1954, pp. 367-74; George H. Williams, "Michael Servetus and a Theology of Nature," *Journal of the Liberal Ministry*, Spring, 1963, pp. 121-29; Hugh Montefiore, "Man's Dominion," *Theology*, 1965, pp. 41-46; and Richard A. Baer, Jr., "Land Misuse: A Theological Concern," *Christian Century*, October 12, 1966, pp. 1239-41, and "Conservation: An Area for the Church's Concern," *Christian Century*, January 8, 1969, pp. 40-43. Santmire's thesis also contains environmental concern, suggesting that today the most adequate "theologian" is not Karl Barth but someone like the naturalist John Muir.

require a careful definition of freedom, something that I shall offer subsequently.

Other minor forces can be thought of, ones that have proved persistent though never achieving decisive influence. There is, for instance, the conservation movement in America, which has fought a long, gallant, bitter, but steadily losing battle to the various man-centered forces, be they economic, social, religious, political, or just plain vindictive. Armed with the disastrous ecological balance sheet, the conservation movement could conceivably at last take the play away from the heretofore winning forces. How close the contest has become has been illustrated in recent years by the way conservationists have achieved a national redwoods park, forestalled the damming of the Grand Canyon, and even brought the Army Corp of Engineers to court for their practices in the Everglades.

Another minor force that could emerge as a major one has to do with the attitude toward science and technology. Once again looking at the list of value orientations, we note that science and secular rationality are there. Applied science is highly esteemed because of its illustrated ability to control the natural order. Yet as the populace becomes more aware of how this control very often turns out to be pollution-producing or depersonalizing, their favor could well be modified. This would bring to the fore a minor theme that has always persisted in connection with applied science. As Williams puts it: "Popular attitudes toward science still contain strong ambivalences. The caricature of the diabolical scientist co-exists with the stereotype of the benevolent laboratory magician." [5] Thus, the negative emphasis could well gain strength. It probably would not cast science in the diabolical role (nor should it), but it could strongly temper the unbridled spirit that has marked technology in many quarters of Western society, and especially American society.

Finally, there is the possibility, though admittedly remote, that the sense of wonder found in men such as Eiseley and other sensitive persons could be more generally recognized and appreciated. What keeps this from being a fanciful suggestion is the presence of a whole subculture that has turned away from the computerized, nonpoetic society that dominates. The Hippies are a judgment upon society; they have exposed it as having excluded much of what differentiates a man from a machine.

However, while the Hippies are a judgment upon society, they are certainly not its corrective. It can be said that they are a bad reaction to a bad action. Theirs is not an ennobling withdrawal or a search for a better dimension of existence. Some have quickly shown themselves to be no more than Western activists in a slightly different form; these are

[5] Robin Williams, *American Society*, p. 455.

the Hippies who have become Yippies. Apart from that, the music that the Hippie culture emphasizes is wild and superficial, and their central focus—drug use—is an extremely dangerous attempt to exceed the limits of the normal, chemically balanced mind. In a world where they protest the number of external forces and stimuli upon them (foisted upon them by the Establishment), they seek out the seemingly thunderous stimuli of various psychedelic excursions. So while the Hippies have in their own way sensed the problem of modern society, their answer to it is neither thoughtful nor constructive; indeed, their answer just creates another problem.

In opposition to this inadequate expression of the Hippies I would forward the idea that what is desperately needed now in Western society is the emergence of a modern asceticism. Now Cox has posed the modern pragmatist as an ascetic because of the way such a person excludes "irrelevant" considerations in order to solve a specialized problem or problems. That person withdraws attention from certain areas in order to concentrate action upon one or a few areas. But that is not at all what I have in mind. Rather, I would emphasize a withdrawal, or at least a reduction, of action in specialized areas in order to give attention to the broad spectrum of interrelated life. This broader view would be the new framework of meaning ("intellectus," as Richardson likes to say) in which the minor views and movements I have reviewed could emerge to a position of dominance. It would not involve a withdrawal from the world [6] in the way Medieval asceticism was, but would simply be a new way of thinking and acting toward and, we can say, *with* the world.

Elements of this new asceticism might eventually be several, but for now I can specify three that are fundamental. These are: (1) restraint, (2) an emphasis upon quality existence, and (3) reverence for life.

The first of these elements is, of course, practically inherent in any concept of asceticism. In a simplified way, it means that in the man-nature relation the ability to say and mean "I can" will not inevitably be followed by the statement "I shall." No longer will the old, undefended argument that men climb mountains because they are there go unchallenged. In the era of restraint the question will be asked as to whether men *should* climb this mountain or that mountain, whether men *should* build this dam or that dam, whether men *should* develop this new product or that new product. And, even more, when the question is asked, the burden of proof will be upon the one proposing the change and not the one who has questions about it. In a day

---

[6] V. A. Demant has written briefly on a "worldly asceticism" in his essay, "Asceticism in the Modern World," which is part of his book, *The Idea of a Natural Order* (Philadelphia: Fortress Press, Facet Books, 1966).

of ecological crisis men who would seriously tamper with natural systems must be able to justify their actions in every way, and most especially, ecologically.

Of course, this element of restraint will have to touch the whole matter of human procreation. If humanity does not quit increasing in size, disaster is sure. And if it is not nutritional disaster, then it will be some other kind, possibly aesthetic or psychological or nuclear. And the responsibility will be upon those who do not restrain their procreation through proper means. The couple that adds to the population (and a population will increase if couples on the average have more than 2.3 children) will be obliged to explain why in the name of both fairness and the public good they brought about such an addition.

Now such a position as this strikes contemporary people as incredibly harsh. Certainly it is unlike anything any previous generation has had to face. But the fact is that the emerging generation now faces the inherent limitations of earthly existence as no other generation has faced them. The forebears of the emerging generation could get away with the idea of a relatively unlimited procreation; the emerging generation cannot. Family limitation, as I speak of it, is a great demand and is harsh, but the severity of it pales in the face of the alternatives.

This whole matter of restraint brings into focus the matter of an adequately defined freedom. And Western man, especially the American, greatly needs such a definition. Robin Williams, when speaking about freedom in America, remarks that "the historical process left its mark in a culturally standardized way of thought and evaluation—a tendency, to think of rights rather than duties."[7] It has been proposed that freedom may be defined by the simple definition, X is free from Y to do Z.[8] In America it may be inferred that only the first two thirds of the formula has been emphasized, especially as regards the natural order. In other words, a person's rights are stressed, but the accompanying responsibilities that could be inferred from the goal of freedom (Z in the formula) are left in dispute, since Z is wholly relative to the agent.

What this indicates is that freedom in America is seen as an end rather than as a means. Importance is put on men being free *from* rather than being free *for*. Possibly in a young nation, with always a new frontier, such a view was permissible, but now, when the biological limitations have become starkly evident, it no longer will do. Freedom can

[7] Robin Williams, *American Society*, p. 446.
[8] This formula is suggested by Dr. John Rawls, Professor of Philosophy at Harvard in his work in social and political philosophy.

no longer be visualized as some vast expanse lying
over against the area of slavery, confinement, limitation, or what you will—the area from which
one must escape in order to reach the other area.
Rather it must be seen as a narrow road that lies
between contrasting areas of slavery, confinement,
and trouble. Thus, for mankind to be mankind it is
true that it must carve out its niche in nature and
from nature so as to escape from being no more
than a beast. But once having done this, mankind
must not make the mistake of equating superiority
to the beast with being un-biological. Mankind must
walk the narrow road that leads between subservience to nature on the one hand and ecological reper-
cussion on the other.

In walking this path it is conceivable that man
might become so acute that he could not only live
in harmony with nature but might find out where he
could truly improve upon it. He could live with nature in a state of what the ecologists call mutualism,
a state of equally benefiting symbiosis. Thus man
would not only be dependent upon nature, but could
even become interdependent, in the sense that the
overall integrity of the biosphere might be kept
in better balance with his informed and benevolent
help.

However, the possibility of interdependence is far
removed at present. What is of concern now is to
keep man from pursuing the direction toward de-

struction that he is presently following. This direction can be altered with the emergence of the new asceticism, with the first emphasis on restraint.

The second emphasis in the new asceticism would be upon quality existence in contrast to the quantity existence that Western man now either has or is convinced he wants. Recalling again the American value-orientations listed at the beginning of this chapter, let us note that the first one is achievement and success, which has come to be spelled out primarily in terms of another value-orientation, material comfort. The means by which success has been attained and material comfort provided has been the unprecedented exploitation of natural systems by Americans, and it is only in the present era that the true cost of quantity existence has appeared. The cost is revealed in such things as the river beds of almost all major cities being little more than sludge ditches, the Great Lakes turning into large polluted ponds, countrysides being raped by strip mining, and sleazy developments and mountains of garbage and refuse beginning to build in the large metropolitan areas.

From the Puritan ideal of thrift and a lack of ostentation, America (and virtually the rest of the world, which she influences) has slipped into the well-known state of (or desire for) conspicuous consumption. The power of the consumption society can be seen in the way that many who protest against it do so not because there is such consumption but because they feel they are not getting their fair share of it. Again, it is only of late, with the emergence of the Hippies, that we have seen a "pure" protest against such consumption, but the Hippies, lacking the Puritan ideal of discipline, degenerate into a worse condition than the society against which they rail.

One of the prime movers of quantity existence is the whole great enterprise of advertising. The new asceticism would involve a resistance to much of modern advertising, not only because of its banality, but because it is realized that any enterprise that continues to support conspicuous consumption hastens the day of ecological reckoning. With a stress on quality existence there would be an emphasis on discrimination, with taste defined not only by what one acquired but also by what one did not acquire. Certainly there would be acquisition, for the new asceticism would not be a world-denying expression; but materialism would now be a concern for what was preserved along with what was acquired.

The result of this new restrained acquisition would be the elimination of what V. A. Demant calls modern Western man's *pleonexia*—his wanting more and more—and would lead to preference for "good food, good houses, good clothes, good furniture over status-enhancing, wealth-flaunting, smartness-flashing acquisitions."[9]

Along with restrained acquisition, however, there would also have to be restrained procreation. Growing, mass society can employ most of its people only if it tolerates many superficial, if not harmful, products and processes. If these were reduced there would be a major economic crisis. Therefore, there must be a reduction in employed persons and consumers to accompany the reduction in consumption. This means population control, with an emphasis upon quality rather than quantity of persons. The emphasis would shift from economies of scale (growing economies, usually involving growing populations) to economies of stabilization, with the impetus for such a shift being the foreboding ecological indexes along with a growing awareness of how gross acquisitiveness leads to superficiality and meaninglessness in persons.

Population control would also be the key to another aspect of quality existence—diversity of setting. The visions of men like Harrison Brown and Daniel Luten are visions of quality. They would lead, as Luten says, to an intensification of consciousness, not via drugs or the worlds of escape produced by television and motion pictures, but by exposure to contrasting natural and social settings. In this world of contrasts the symbolism and sig-

[9] Demant, *The Idea of a Natural Order*, p. 39.

nificance of all life's expressions could be realized
by man in a healthy, balanced context. Such a context can emerge only if men quit putting emphasis
upon their numbers and shift over to the development and cultivation of the responsible individual
member of the species.

An emphasis upon quality existence shades over
into the third element of the new asceticism, a reverence for life. This phrase, made famous by Al-
bert Schweitzer, would come to mean an appreciation for *any* expression of life, based on scientific,
aesthetic, and religious considerations. The cultivation of an individual, therefore, would involve his
coming to realize that, say, a tree is an indispensable part of the photosynthetic process, a thing of
beauty, and the handiwork of God. Reverence for
life would be a central concept of what could become an emerging environmental ethic, a system
of behavior standing in sharp contrast to the anthropocentric ethic that we presently have.[10] This ethic
would encompass the relations of man to nature,

[10] A pertinent example of anthropocentric bias in Christian
social ethics comes from Richard Fagley's pioneering work on
the population problem. At the beginning of his book Fagley
wrote that the problem "is a temporal problem in the sense that
it stems not from the fact of human increase but from the
rate of that increase in relation to the tempo of economic and
social development, and the absorptive capacity of varying civilizations." *The Population Explosion and Christian Responsibility*
(New York: Oxford University Press, 1960), p. 3. In Fagley's
view, "overpopulation can be defined only in relation to the available resources" (*ibid.*, p. 19), a typical man-centered sentiment.

thus finally satisfying the complaint of Aldo Leopold.[11] Indeed one of the principles of an environmental ethic could well be some form of a principle Leopold himself expressed. The principle he proposed was: "A thing is right when it tends to preserve the integrity, stability and beauty of the biotic community. It is wrong when it tends otherwise."[12]

So, reverence for life would place ethical considerations in a broader perspective. This would result in both a curtailment of some of man's activity (lest he disrupt the biotic community in a variety of ways) and would diminish the present, bloated view that man has of himself. Reverence for life involves a diminution of emphasis upon just some life, that is, human life, so that with it the god of anthropocentrism would sway and finally fall off its presently elevated pedestal.

However, the loss of anthropocentrism need not demean man; indeed, it would benefit him. It would insure him the kind of environment where his life would be not only viable but also stimulating because of its diversity. In addition, and somewhat paradoxically, as man shifted some of the emphasis away from himself and projected it more upon a reverence for all life, that reverence, in turn, would be projected back into man and leave him a better creature than when he started. Anthropocentric man

[11] Cf. *supra*, p. 92.
[12] Leopold, *A Sand County Almanac*, p. 240.

is also pragmatic man, and his modes of thought
run toward efficiency, practicality, and utility. What
they do not run toward is reverence.

So, anthropocentric man, even though placing man
in the center of things, does not deal with his species
in a spirit of reverence. He will build a pinball
machine of a world without ever asking whether
such a project violates something in man. He will
channel men into a multi-digited existence and see
no relevance to a question as to whether he should
do such a thing. He will quickly agree to abortion
on demand as an answer to the population question
without ever pausing to reflect upon the fact that
abortion on demand marks the same kind of narrow-
answer approach that has brought humanity to
the brink of ecological disaster in the first place.

Over against this, reverence for life creates in
a person a strong sense of biological balance and
proportion, a symbiotic conscience, and, more to the
point, a demand that every life form be given consideration beyond the measure of utility. When applied to man, this means that the person in a "back-
ward" or "underdeveloped" culture will no longer
be judged somehow insufficient, but be seen as an
expression of humanity of value in its own mode.
And as to the question of abortion, the practice
will be rejected in all but the most extreme cases[13]

[13] There are cases where abortion must be seriously considered,
that is, in connection with incest, rape, extreme danger to the

because fetal life, though small and undeveloped, will not be seen as therefore unimportant. Reverence for all life, with that life seen as a gestalt, does not question population control, but it does require that it be carried out responsibly, that is, by the avoidance of the creation of new life, and not by the destruction of life already created. With reverence for life as a criterion for judgment, it can be asked whether solving the population problem by abortion is on any higher ethical plane than solving it by means of forced starvation or nuclear weapons.

Having taken a look at modern asceticism, we are faced with the question as to where it gets inserted into the society. In America at least (and what happens in America will have repercussions around the world) the answer is the churches. This answer is arrived at by two different means.

The first of these means is by a process of elimination. Looking at the other large social institutions in America, we can ask whether any of them are capable of bringing about a shift from a subjugation to a symbiotic mentality toward nature. Can they establish value-orientations that tend toward

life of the mother, and, possibly, where the mother has certain diseases during pregnancy. But I would contend that these are the causes for a minority of abortions, and that the majority has to do with matters of inconvenience and negligence. In dealing with abortion the reader surmises, of course, that I define human life as beginning with conception—the point that initiates the continuum that runs through prenatal development, birth, childhood, youth, maturity, and that ends with death.

a harmonious relation between man and the natural order? It would appear that the answer is no.

Government can have some impact in this area, but in America, government, for all the fear of its autonomy, is still a reflection of what the populace in general thinks. Moreover, as some have pointed out, the American government is morally neutral is many areas and leaves to other institutions the establishment of moral identities. In this condition the government becomes a spectator watching the struggle over value-orientations, a spectator who will in the end join with the winner, whoever that may be.

It is true that the schools could be a place where value-orientations favorable to the natural order might be cultivated. However, as one observer has pointed out: "Our schools no longer transmit values for the most part; they regard it as their job to question values." This position, the writer says, has resulted because the schools have cracked under the strain of assuming traditional moral teaching shifted to it in large part by the family and the churches. Thus the schools have become part of what the writer, using a borrowed term, says is an "adversary culture." [14] The schools are playing the same role as the Hippies (though still in a less bizarre way); they protest because of the problem,

[14] Irving Kristol, "The Old Politics, the New Politics, the *New*, New Politics," *New York Times Magazine*, November 24, 1968, p. 179.

but they have no constructive positions that could correct it.

The family, one of the two institutions from which moral authority was shifted to the schools, in many individual instances still has enough authority left whereby a sense of the new asceticism could be established. Even considering the exceptions, however, the fact remains that the family is more and more eclipsed by the contemporary giant society, its authority having been eroded by the diverse activities of the different family members as well as by the persistent disruption of the mass media. Besides, the question remains as to how families would be informed of the new asceticism; it is inconceivable that they would arrive at it individually.

This, then, leaves the churches as the major force in society that could bring about a significant shift in value-orientations. Now, as has been mentioned, it is true that the churches have shifted much of their moral authority away. Nevertheless, at least in America, the aura of the moral instructor still is around the churches, and a forthright effort on their part to establish a symbiotic consciousness could have a significant effect. This contention is lent credence by looking at another great area of concern, the civil rights movement. For all their tardiness, once even some of the churches gave support to that movement there was an improvement in the attitude of many as to its correctness.

Another way of deciding that it is the churches that must insert the new asceticism into society comes from the positive advantages they hold over other institutions in their attempt to do this. For instance, the churches, though being the custodians of the dominion as dominance view (again, derived largely from Genesis), nevertheless have the minor theme of man-nature harmony in their literature and background, and this minor theme could be forwarded. While the rest of Western society has adopted the anthropocentric position from Christianity and then has been left largely with no rationale for an alternative, the churches have in their midst the corrective for the very view for which they are historically responsible. Thus, even while they maintain the view that man is made in the image of God they can also assert the biblical position that man is made of dust, that is, that he is earthly. Even while they speak of Jesus as the savior of men, they can also stress that Jesus was one who spoke of lilies of the field and "insignificant" creatures like sparrows. Even while maintaining the traditional meanings of stewardship they can emphasize that man must also deal with the earth as a steward, with an emphasis upon biological harmony and a new era of human restraint.

Of course, to do this the churches must accomplish a large shift in their ethical thinking. Above all, they must re-evaluate what it means to be relevant. "Relevance" in the 1960's came to have a very narrow meaning. Ethically it meant little more than concern over the Vietnam War along with social and economic concern over the closely related problems of race and poverty. Within this narrow spectrum the great emphasis was (and is) on human rights, human release, human freedom. Without denying for a moment the validity and nobility of much of this emphasis, the fact remains that enormous concerns have been ignored or given only perfunctory attention because of the attention given to "relevant" issues. Foremost among these is the relation of man and the natural order. Indeed, because of the narrowness of scope some truly relevant considerations have been shunted aside in regard to the issues of war, poverty, and discrimination. For instance, in discussions concerning war and poverty it is not often said that these problems are exacerbated because nations and families simply have too many citizens and members. In the grip of anthropocentric bias too many Christian ethicists have simply been unwilling to admit that humanity continues to worsen its own social condition because of its undisciplined breeding.

In the decade of the 1970's there must emerge in Christian ethical thinking the broader view that will encompass nature, a view that will at the same time put man in his proper place. This thinking will go beyond the humanistic emphasis that prevails so much today, and will reassert the value of nonhuman life forms. It will dwell on the fact that man is not only the object of God's grace but also the recipient of his judgment. This means that a new stress on human responsibility will arise, resulting in a confrontation with the popular American idea of freedom.[15] Man-centered views such as those of Teilhard, Cox, and Richardson, for all their imagination, will be set aside because it will be realized that they are accommodating positions that lead only to a confrontation with the God who unifies the world.

With God understood this way we have another good reason why the churches are the ones to emphasize the new asceticism. With the sovereign God the churches have in their possession the one reference that can meaningfully shift attention away from man. Understanding God as far more than the deity whose only concern is man, the churches, better than other institutions, can have good reason to insist that man must turn in a new direction if he is to avoid disaster. Theocentrism will no longer be once removed, as it is with Cox and Richardson; rather it will be present in every concern and, most especially, in the realm of the biological. Man has "conquered" the biosphere because there was seemingly nothing in the created realm to stop his subjugating surge. With God thrust into the picture as an immanent

[15] *Supra,* pp. 147-48.

power of judgment (as well as one of beneficence) the conquest mentality can be effectively challenged.

Moreover, there is a ready audience to whom and through whom the challenge can be transmitted. In America, in spite of its increasingly secular nature, 40 to 50 percent of the adult population is in church on a given Sunday. A regular exposition of the new asceticism to them could have a great impact on the country and could conceivably bring about the shift in value-orientations that is required. The churches could emerge from their ethical parochialism and, armed with empirical and aesthetic, as well as biblical and theological data, could lead the country, and through it the entire planet, back from the brink of ecological disaster on which it presently teeters. This would be a world-saving endeavor, but that, in one form or another, has always been the mission of the Savior's churches.

This endeavor would be carried out by bringing about changes in attitude, that most difficult of tasks. In saying this I am not implying that action in areas of ecological relevance is not to be continued; all conservation efforts must be supported. However, the ultimate task is not defensive measures that hold the line against the traditional exploitation by Western man. The task is to replace that exploitative nature with a harmonic one. This involves nothing less than a conversion, but here again the churches are best equipped to carry out this sort of thing, since conversion has always been a part of their belief and makeup.

The time in which the conversion must take place is not long. The human race probably has no more than a generation left in which to decide whether it will live in a diversified, balanced world or one either biologically devastated or imperialistically controlled in order to avoid biological devastation. This means that environmental theology and its concomitant, environmental ethics, must emerge. It means that now is the time for the proclamation of the new asceticism through which man at last becomes biologically sophisticated and materially reverent. The time is now; a failure to proceed properly insures a future that is bleak.

Bibliography

BOOKS

Bonifazi, Conrad. *A Theology of Things.* Philadelphia: Lippincott, 1967.

Borgstrom, Georg. *The Hungry Planet.* New York: Macmillan, 1965. Collier Books Rev. Ed., 1967.

Brown, Harrison. *The Challenge of Man's Future.* New York: Viking Press, Compass Ed., 1956.

Carson, Rachel. *Silent Spring.* Greenwich, Conn.: Fawcett Crest Books, 1964.

Clarke, George L. *Elements of Ecology.* Rev. ed. New York: Wiley, 1966.

Commoner, Barry. *Science and Survival.* New York: The Viking Press, Compass Ed., 1967.

Cox, Harvey. *The Secular City.* New York: Macmillan, 1965.
———. *On Not Leaving It to the Snake.* New York: Macmillan, 1967.

Demant, V. A. *The Idea of a Natural Order.* Philadelphia: Fortress Press, Facet Books, 1966.

Ehrlich, Paul. *The Population Bomb.* New York: Ballentine Books, 1968.

Eiseley, Loren C. *The Immense Journey.* New York: Random House, Vintage Books, 1957.

————. *The Mind as Nature.* New York: Harper, 1962.

————. *Francis Bacon and the Modern Dilemma.* Lincoln: University of Nebraska Press, 1962.

————. *The Firmament of Time.* New York: Atheneum, 1960.

Fagley, Richard M. *The Population Explosion and Christian Responsibility.* New York: Oxford University Press, 1960.

Freedman, Ronald, ed. *Population: The Vital Revolution.* Garden City, N.Y.: Doubleday, Anchor Books, 1964.

Henderson, Lawrence J. *The Fitness of the Environment.* Intro. George Wald. Boston: Beacon Press [1913], 1966.

Huxley, Aldous. *Brave New World Revisited.* New York: Bantam Books, 1960.

Leopold, Aldo. *A Sand County Almanac: With Other Essays on Conservation from Round River.* New York: Oxford University Press, 1949; enl. ed., 1966.

Marsh, George Perkins. *Man and Nature: Or, Physical Geography as Modified by Human Action.* Ed., David Lowenthal. Cambridge: Harvard University Press [1864], 1965.

Moule, C. F. D. *Man and Nature in the New Testament.* Philadelphia: Fortress Press, Facet Books, 1967.

Mudd, Stuart, ed. *The Population Crisis and the Use of World Resources.* Bloomington: Indiana University Press, 1964.

Nash, Roderick. *Wilderness and the American Mind.* New Haven: Yale University Press, 1967.

Niebuhr, H. Richard. *Radical Monotheism and Western Culture.* Lincoln: Univ. of Nebraska Press, 1960.

Odum, Eugene P. *Ecology.* New York: Holt, Rinehart & Winston, 1963.

Paddock, William and Paddock, Paul. *Famine—1975!* Boston: Little, Brown, 1967.

Raven, Charles E. *Natural Religion and Christian Theology.* Cambridge: The University Press, 1953. Chapters I, II, X.

Richardson, Herbert W. *Toward an American Theology.* New York: Harper, 1967.

Rust, E. C. *Nature and Man in Biblical Thought.* London: Lutterworth Press, 1953.

Sinnott, Edmund W. *The Bridge of Life.* New York: Simon and Schuster, 1966.

Teilhard de Chardin, Pierre. *The Phenomenon of Man.* Trans. by Bernard Wall. New York: Harper, Torchbook Ed., 1965.

Thorpe, W. H. *Science, Man and Morals.* Ithaca: Cornell University Press, 1966.

Williams, Robin M., Jr. *American Society.* 2nd ed. rev. New York: Knopf, 1967. Chapter XI.

ARTICLES

Baer, Richard A., Jr. "Land Misuse: A Theological Concern." *Christian Century,* October 12, 1966, pp. 1239-41.

———. "Conservation: An Arena for the Church's Concern." *Christian Century,* January 8, 1969, pp. 40-43.

Calhoun, John C. "Population Density and Social Pathology." *Scientific American,* February, 1962.

Drury, William H. "Are Conservation Values Limited to Esthetics?" *Environmental Hazards,* pp. 162-71. Reprinted from The New England Journal of Medicine.

Dyck, Arthur J. "Religious Factors in the Population Problem." *The Religious Situation,* ed. Donald Cutler. Boston: Beacon Press, 1968.

Eiseley, Loren C. "An Evolutionist Looks at Modern Man." *Saturday Evening Post,* April 26, 1958.

———. "Man: The Lethal Factor." *American Scientist,* 1963, pp. 71-83.

Luten, Daniel B. "How Dense Can People Be?" Reprint from the *Sierra Club Bulletin,* December, 1963.

Lyle, David. "The Human Race Has, Maybe, Thirty-five Years Left." *Esquire,* September, 1967.

Lyon, David L. "An Ecologist's View of the Population Problem." *The Living Wilderness,* Spring and Summer, 1967.

McHarg, Ian. "The Place of Nature in the City of Man." Reprint from *The Annals of the American Academy of Political and Social Science,* March, 1964.

Milby, T. H. "People and the World as Subject." *Religion in Life,* 1962, pp. 238-43.

Montefiore, Hugh. "Man's Dominion." *Theology,* 1965, pp. 41-46.

Sears, Paul B. "Utopia and the Living Landscape." *Daedalus,* Spring, 1965, pp. 474-86.

Simpson, George Gaylord. "The Crisis in Biology." *The American Scholar*, Summer, 1967, pp. 363-77.

Sittler, Joseph, Jr. "A Theology for Earth." *The Christian Scholar*, June, 1954, pp. 367-74.

White, Lynn, Jr. "The Historical Roots of Our Ecologic Crisis." *Science*, March 10, 1967, pp. 1203-07.

Williams, George H. "Michael Servetus and a Theology of Nature." *Journal of the Liberal Ministry*, Fall, 1964, pp. 121-29.

UNPUBLISHED MATERIAL

Eiseley, Loren C. Transcript of the television program, "The House We Live In," WCAU-TV, Philadelphia, Pennsylvania, February 5, 1961.

McHarg, Ian, "Ecological Determinism." Background paper for Landscape Architecture III, University of Pennsylvania, n.d.

———. "Man and Environment." Background paper for Landscape Architecture III, University of Pennsylvania, n.d.

———. "Values, Process and Form." Paper for the Second International Symposium of the Smithsonian Institution, "The Quality of Man's Environment," Washington, D.C., February, 1967.

Ping, Charles L. "Numbers and Quality." Special background papers for the Alma College American Assembly on the Population Dilemma, April 6-9, 1967.

Revelle, Roger. "Pollution and Cities." Background paper for Environmental Health 1a, b, Harvard School of Public Health, December, 1966.

Santmire, Paul H. "Creation and Nature: A Study of the Doctrine of Nature with Special Attention to Karl Barth's Doctrine of Creation." Unpublished Th.D. thesis, Harvard University, 1966.

GOVERNMENT DOCUMENTS

The Environmental Pollution Panel, President's Science Advisory Committee. *Restoring the Quality of Our Environment*. The White House. Washington, D.C.: Government Printing Office, December, 1965.

The Task Force on Environmental Health and Related Problems.

A Strategy for a Livable Environment. A report to the Secretary of Health, Education and Welfare. Washington, D.C.: Government Printing Office, June, 1967.

U. S. Department of the Interior. *Quest for Quality.* Conservation Yearbook #1. Washington, D.C.: Government Printing Office, 1965.

————. *The Population Challenge.* Conservation Yearbook #2. Washington, D.C.: Government Printing Office, 1966.

Index